Praying with Purpose

TAKING YOUR PRAYERS FROM *Vague* TO *Victorious*

By Deborah Haddix

Warner Press, Inc.
Warner Press and "Warner Press" logo are trademarks of Warner Press, Inc.
Praying with Purpose: Taking Your Prayers from Vague to Victorious Second Edition
Copyright ©2018 by Deborah Haddix
Cover design and layout Copyright ©2018 Warner Press, Inc.
All rights reserved.

All Scripture quotations, unless otherwise indicated, are taken from The Holy Bible, English Standard Version® (ESV®), copyright ©2001 by Crossway, a publishing ministry of Good News Publishers. Used by permission. All rights reserved.

Scripture quotations marked NASB are taken from the New American Standard Bible®, © 1960, 1962, 1963, 1968,1971, 1972, 1973, 1975, 1977, 1995 by The Lockman Foundation. Used by permission. (www.Lockman.org)

Scripture quotations marked NIV are taken from The Holy Bible, New International Version®. NIV®. Copyright © 1973, 1978, 1984, 2011 by Biblica, Inc.® Used by permission. All rights reserved worldwide.

Scripture quotations marked NIV1984 are taken from HOLY BIBLE, NEW INTERNATIONAL VERSION®. NIV®. Copyright © 1973, 1978, 1984 by International Bible Society. Used by permission of Zondervan Publishing House. All rights reserved.

Scripture quotations marked NKJV are taken from the New King James Version. Copyright © 1982 by Thomas Nelson, Inc. Used by permission. All rights reserved.

Scripture quotations marked TLB are taken from The Living Bible copyright © 1971 by Tyndale House Foundation. Used by permission. All rights reserved.

All rights reserved. No part of this publication may be reproduced, stored in a retrieval system, or transmitted in any form or by any means—electronic, mechanical, photocopy, recording, or any other—except for brief quotations in printed reviews, without the prior permission of the publisher.

Requests for information should be sent to:
Warner Press Inc
2902 Enterprise Dr
P.O. Box 2499
Anderson, IN 46013
www.warnerpress.org

Editors: Karen Rhodes, Tammy Tilley
Designer: Curtis Corzine
Layout: Katie Miller

ISBN 978-1-68434-088-0
E Pub 978-1-68434-093-4

Printed in USA

CONTENTS

PART 1: Our Most Powerful Tool 7
- Our Job 9
- Our Battle 10
- Our Weapon 12
- Our Roadblocks 14
- Our Encouragement 19
- Our Legacy 21
- Our Intention 25
- Our Call 27

PART 2: Shaping Tools 31
- Prayer Journal 32
- Monthly Prayer Calendars 40
- Praying Scripture 41
- Prayer Box 43
- Prayer Log 45

PART 3: Detailing Tools 51

Prayer Suggestions for...
- Your Husband 52
- Children/Grandchildrens' Future 58
- Stages of Life 59
- Your Child's Future Mate 62
- Engaged Couple 63
- Friend 64
- Adult Children 65
- Aging Parents 66
- Your Pastor 67
- The Church 68
- Seasons of Transition 69
- Seasons of Anxiety 70

Praying Scriptures for...
- Yourself 71
- Godly Character 73
- Praise 76
- Singles 80
- Wives 83
- Marriage 87
- Your Children 90
- Grandchildren 95
- Seasons of Waiting 98

PART 1

Our Most Powerful Tool

I know prayer is important. I grew up in the church. I've heard it all my life. I serve on the prayer team at Christian Grandparenting Network where part of my role is to encourage other grandparents in their prayer life. I am a wife, mother, and grandparent—aware of the constant spiritual battle raging around my family.

Yet, I have struggled for years and often continue to struggle in my prayer life. Sometimes the struggle is with my schedule and making sure prayer happens. Other times my struggle is with WHAT to pray. I will admit to succumbing on more than one occasion to praying the VAGUE, "Dear Lord, please be with my grandchildren today," or "Help my husband have a good day."

In recent years God has brought the word INTENTIONAL across my path more than once. I've learned that when He keeps bringing something to me, He has something for me. What does it mean to be INTENTIONAL about my use of time? About being present to those I love? About spending time in God's Word? About prayer?

To the people in my life, my prayers are vital. How can I be more INTENTIONAL to see that time in prayer actually happens? How can I take my prayers from VAGUE to VICTORIOUS?

Those are the thoughts and questions behind this book—a resource for those who face my same struggles. In these pages you will find ideas for getting past the busyness and getting to prayer—practical ideas that can be implemented quickly and easily. In Part Two, you will also discover several methods for using your unique God-wiring in your prayers. Choose one or two and allow them to draw you into your prayer time. Finally, Part Three is full of Prayer Guides—resources full of ideas for WHAT to pray.

I pray that the ideas and tools in this resource will help you as they have helped me to pray more passionately for others. My hope is that you will have all the tools you need right there in your hands so you can begin today. No matter your role or life stage, you are busy, and it is my desire to help equip and empower you to live out your God-given design in the midst of that busy.

Finally, as you read this book, my prayer is that you will be challenged to pray strategically and deliberately for those who hold a special place in your heart. Isaiah 44:3 states, *I will pour my Spirit upon your offspring, and my blessing on your descendants.* God still promises to pour out His Spirit and His blessing on our descendants. Isn't this ultimately what we want for our family members and others we love?

This book is all about the most powerful tool God has given us—prayer. May you discover that the prayer tools you use today will impact your loved ones for all of eternity. May you commit to intentional, consistent, and specific prayer for others. May you leave a godly legacy to the generations to follow—one that points them to Him. And may you do it through VICTORIOUS prayer.

Our Job

Being involved in the lives of others has many benefits. Watching those we love grow, both physically and spiritually, is fun. Coming up with things to do and see together provides opportunity for creative thinking. Sharing hobbies and interests adds depth and dimension to our lives and relationships. God's plan for community is one of rich blessing.

But as is the case with most things, along with the pleasure comes responsibility. Prayer is one of those responsibilities, and it is one of great magnitude.

Prayer is power. In her Bible study, *Live a Praying Life*, Jennifer Kennedy Dean states, "Our prayers allow God to accomplish His purpose in and through lives."[2] In other words, it is through our prayers that God is moved to shape the lives of others. Prayer produces effect. When you pray for your loved ones, you unleash eternal impacting power on their lives.

One of the greatest investments you will ever make into the lives of others is the investment of prayer. Faithful intercessory prayer will help your spouse, child, grandchild, or anyone else you care deeply for, live a life worthy of the Lord, grow in knowledge of Him, and have power to joyfully endure life's trials. Bottom line—your prayers will have an eternal impact. Begin now. It's never too late.

> "Prayer does not equip us for greater works—prayer is the greater work."[1]
>
> Oswald Chambers

Our Battle

Prayer is necessary and our most powerful weapon in the battle for souls, the souls of our children, grandchildren, and others in our circle of influence.

Just stop and look at our world today. Children of all ages are growing up in a culture where sin is rampant: acting out, rebellion, alcoholism, drug addiction, negative peer pressure, gangs, pornography. It is a fact we simply cannot turn a blind eye to. Satan wants nothing more than the hearts and minds of our children.

Prayer is the key. Through prayer Satan's schemes and powers toward our children can be stopped. Through prayer God's power and provision for them can flow fully.

The effective prayer of a righteous man can accomplish much (James 5:16, NASB).

Ephesians 6:12 describes the battle, *For we do not wrestle against flesh and blood, but against the rulers, against the authorities, against the cosmic powers over this present darkness, against the spiritual forces of evil in the heavenly places.*

God hears your prayers—lone grandmother, mother, friend—when you kneel in prayer on behalf of a struggling loved one.

And this is the confidence that we have toward him, that if we ask anything according to his will he hears us (1 John 5:14).

Never underestimate the power of two or more. Remember, the battle you are fighting is one of eternal impact. If both you and your spouse are believers in Christ, consider devoting some of your "together" praying time to that young family member who doesn't yet have a personal relationship with Christ. Unite with other family members in praying for a wayward child, or ask a friend or two to join you in praying for those that God has placed upon your heart.

Again I say to you, if two of you agree on earth about anything they ask, it will be done for them by my Father in heaven. For where two or three are gathered in my name, there am I among them (Matthew 18:19-20).

No matter who or how old your loved ones, they need your prayers for protection and direction. They also need your prayers for their parents, peers, and other influencers. Start now. Bathe those precious souls in prayer. God sees. God hears. God answers.

"*Through prayer,*

the enemy's schemes are thwarted.

Through prayer,

the powers, principalities, and authorities of Satan's realm are stopped cold.

Through prayer,

all the power and provision of God flows into the lives of His people."[3]

Jennifer Kennedy Dean

Our Weapon

> "Persevering and believing prayer means a strong and an abundant life."[4]
>
> Andrew Murray

God has gifted us with a powerful resource—prayer. Through prayer He invites us to bring all our concerns about our loved ones directly to Him. Prayer is more than important. It is vital.

We love. We love those God has placed in our family and those He has brought into our lives in other ways. Most times love is glorious and amazing; however, sometimes our love can become the impetus for such things as worry, anxiety, and fear.

Prayer allows us to release to God what we cannot control ourselves—the circumstances and situations that trigger our worries, anxieties, and fears. Additionally, when we are tempted to become angry or unforgiving, prayer enables us to fill our hearts with compassion. Prayer can even empower a person to speak the truth to another when it would be easier to remain silent.

If there are people in your life who are choosing to live disobedient, rebellious, unbiblical lifestyles, or following destructive paths, it is imperative that you press on in prayer. Prayer is the most powerful tool we can offer on their behalf. Tired? Weary? Sleepless nights? Lost heart? Don't give up. Keep praying. God is up to something. God tells us to ask and to keep on asking, to seek and to keep on seeking, to knock and knock loudly (see Matthew 7:7). He is in the business of breaking down strongholds. He will answer. Releasing those we love to God opens the way for Him to do His work. We can trust God to continue what He has begun in the lives of our loved ones.

Yes, prayer is a powerful resource. It even has the power to close those nasty gaps that tend to cause rifts in our relationships. When we engage in consistent, intentional, specific prayer, our focus is directed toward the person for whom we are praying. Rather than sweating the small stuff, we tune in to real needs. Generational gaps dissipate.

Prayer also closes geographical gaps. No matter how far away your loved one, the number of miles between seems to shrink as continued prayers are offered on their behalf. And prayer makes it much easier to reconnect when time or distance has kept you apart.

As you consistently sit in the presence of the Lord in prayer for others, you will find that you are drawn closer not only to them but also to Him. Your spirit will be nourished, and you will be changed.

"Prayer does change things, all kinds of things. But the most important thing it changes is us. As we engage in this communion with God more deeply and come to know the One with whom we are speaking more intimately, that growing knowledge of God reveals to us all the more brilliantly who we are and our need to change in conformity to Him. Prayer changes us profoundly."[5] R.C. Sproul

You may pray and pray for a specific situation in the life of another and not "see" any change. Rest assured, God is at work in the life of the one for whom you pray, and He is at work in you.

Open your hands. Let go as you lay down your expectations and your own ways of wanting God to work.

For my thoughts are not your thoughts, neither are your ways my ways, declares the Lord (Isaiah 55:8).

Peace will grow in your heart as you release the ones you love to God Almighty. When your impulse is to step in and try to take control of a hard situation, learn instead to stop, take a breath, and go to the Lord in prayer. Rather than assuming the role of "fixer," allow God to work freely in the lives of those you love. As you grow in this area, you will experience, more and more, the power of His peace.

Prayer is the key.

Our Roadblocks

Time

Let's just be honest with one another. We are all busy. No matter our season of life, the proverbial plates are spinning all at the same time in every direction, and we're simply trying to keep from dropping one.

Student, mom of toddlers, father who coaches youth sports, parent of teens, grandparent, whatever your season it's the same scenario, just different plates.

We grasp to varying degrees the power of prayer. We are aware of things we want to pray about, and we acknowledge that prayer changes lives. Many times we can't find the energy or the time to pray. There just don't seem to be enough hours in our day.

The first step in "finding the time" to pray is to remember the importance and power of prayer. Make it a priority—the plate that must be given your daily attention.

Next, examine your life. One way to be consistent in prayer is to pray as you live. Track your schedule for a day or two. Take into consideration your daily routines and obligations. Driving, running errands, exercising, walking the dog, gardening, showering, and even brushing your teeth are opportunities for prayer. Study your list. Determine one or two consistent activities in your schedule where you can attach prayer. A bonus of praying as you live is that your chosen daily activity, whether it be your morning coffee or folding the laundry, serves as a reminder to pray.

Another way to make time for prayer in a busy life is to discover a way of praying that connects naturally to your God-given wiring. We tend to make time for the things we enjoy. Are you a naturalist? Pray as you take a walk or savor a visit to your nearby park. Contemplative? Find a quiet spot for some meditative prayer. Ascetic? Pray in Color (see page 37).

Speaking of praying in color, if your desire is to draw away from the activity of daily life when you pray for your loved ones, but you need help with staying focused, use one of the ideas in the Shaping Tools Section to help.

No matter how you decide to make prayer a priority and fit it into your daily life, know that it's all about routine. Consider your lifestyle and your personality. Find a way to make prayer part of your everyday activity. Begin today to establish your prayer routine.

Content

Whether due to our busier-than-should-be schedules or all the details we are trying to keep track of in our minds, many of us have at times fallen victim to praying very vague and general prayers both for others and for ourselves. In the clamor of our day, we quickly spout off a, "God, bless my grandchildren, protect them, and help them to have a good day," or "Lord, be with me today." Then we're off. While there's nothing at all wrong with a quick breath prayer, sometimes more is needed. I know that personally I have experienced feelings of frustration and lack of peace because of my own vague prayers.

Praying specifically is biblical.

Elijah was a man with a nature like ours, and he prayed fervently that it might not rain, and for three years and six months it did not rain on the earth. Then he prayed again, and heaven gave rain, and the earth bore its fruit (James 5:17-18).

Elijah was a man who prayed very specific prayers.

Our loved ones need so much more than the occasional, "…and bless my children, Lord." It's time we followed the example of Elijah given to us in the Bible. We need to pray specifically.

One way to pray specifically is to ask. Ask the person you are praying for to share their prayer needs with you. If they don't live nearby, ask them to share by phone or email. You might even try mailing them a note, asking them to share their prayer requests. If they do live nearby, ask in person or show them your prayer journal and ask if they have anything they would like for you to add. If the children you are praying for are too young to share their needs, consider asking their parents for input so you may pray more specifically.

New channels of communication can be opened with others when you ask how you

> "In the end the way you'll best learn to pray is by praying. We can read about it all day long, but at the end of it all, you'll just need to close your eyes and pray. There are no experts in prayer; we are all learning, all growing, all reaching for the Lord."[6]
>
> Tim Challies

can pray for them. When those in your circle of family and friends know they can count on you to pray for them, they feel valued.

Aside from asking people their prayer needs directly, I believe the best source for praying specifically is the Bible. Pray Scripture.

Personalize your Scripture prayers by inserting the name of your loved one into the verse. When you pray Scripture, you unleash the supernatural power of God into the life of the person you are praying for. Pray according to God's Word, and you will be praying in line with His will. Best of all, praying God's Word will enable you to pray with His power, direction, and wisdom. As you pray Scripture, you will begin to pray with more confidence and boldness.

If you would love to pray Scripture but are unsure where to begin, try praying the prayers of the apostle Paul which can be found in Ephesians 1:15-23, Ephesians 3:14-21, Philippians 1:9-11, and Colossians 1:9-12. Or pray any of the Psalms—the 91st Psalm is a great place to begin. There are many other Scriptures that can be personalized as you pray. For additional ideas, see any of the Scripture-based resources located in the Detailing Tools Section of this book.

For other prayer specifics, consider the needs and daily life of your family member or friend. Pray for their needs—love, acceptance, and security. When praying for children, pray for the family they are being raised in. If it's a young mom or dad you are praying for, pray for the family they are shepherding. Pray for godly character, relationships, and personal struggles.

One of the most important things we can pray for concerning those we love is to pray for God's will in their lives. Our love for them can often lead us to pray that God will keep them from any discouragement, disappointment, or pain. We just don't want anything bad to happen to the precious people in our lives. We call it protection, but in reality, this is a control issue on our part. As difficult as it is, we need to remember that God often uses discouragement, disappointment, and pain to mature His children in Him. The very circumstance we long to shield our loved one from may, in fact, be the very way the Lord is helping them learn to trust Him—the conduit for His blessings poured out upon them. Letting go is not easy, but we must let God do the holding of our precious ones when we cannot.

When praying specifically, don't forget to pray for the future of the ones for whom you are praying. Lift up their college education or vocational training, their future spouse and marriage, their family and the raising of their children, their occupation, their ministry, and their retirement years. Pray that the individuals on your prayer list will discover their dreams. God has created each one for a unique purpose. Our prayers might include asking that our family members and friends be motivated to pursue their God-given dreams and to trust Him to provide the resources. Again, take care always to pray according to God's will and not from selfishness. For example, when praying for a child or grandchild's future spouse, our desire may be to concentrate on praying for the "perfect" spouse; however, we should be careful to pray that this future mate will become all that he or she can be for God.

In whatever way you choose to pray specifically for others, your primary prayer for each one should be that they will come to realize how much God loves them. Ask that the persons you are praying for come to know that God will always be there for them and pray that they will accept Jesus Christ as their personal Savior. Pray that they will love God with all their heart, soul, mind, and strength. Also pray that they grow spiritually, and that they are discerning in all their choices.

It is my prayer that your love may abound more and more, with knowledge and all discernment, so that you may approve what is excellent, and so be pure and blameless for the day of Christ, filled with the fruit of righteousness that comes through Jesus Christ, to the glory and praise of God (Philippians 1:9-11).

I love so many of the thoughts in the following list of "specifics." These ideas are taken from the article, "10 Things I Prayed for My Children and Grandchildren Today" by Pat Layton; however, the specifics can be prayed for anyone.

- Thank God that your grandchildren [or whoever it is you are praying for] know Christ or pray that they will come to know Him.

- Pray they will commit their lives to Christ and be filled with the Holy Spirit.

- They will recognize that Jesus is The Name Above all Names.

- Each will grasp and understand how far, how wide, how deep is the love of Christ.

- That your grandchild [child, or other] will trust Him alone.

- Pray they will lean not unto their own understanding.

- Know Him intimately: His names, His Word, His will, His heart.

- Will take the time each day to pray and to praise Him.

- Know who they are in Christ.

- That each will know their identity is rooted in Christ alone.

- Be secure in Him.

- Have Christ-centered confidence and worth.

- Be protected from the evil one by the blood of Jesus Christ.

- Guard their thoughts and minds.

- Pray that each will receive God's love as more than enough.

- Love the Word of God.

- Possess an increasing, unquenchable love for God's Word.

- That they will know God's Word so that when the enemy whispers his lies in their ears, they will hear His voice saying, "This is the way—walk here."

- Hate sin.

- Love holiness and righteousness.

- Press daily for Spirit-Filled living—Love, Joy, Peace, Patience, Gentleness, Self-Control, Kindness.

- Give one another the grace that God has extended to each of us.

- Grow daily in spiritual maturity and grace, built on the foundation of Jesus.

- That God would build them in love, faith, spiritual strength, and thankfulness.

- Pray for God to "Father" your [loved one].

- *I have no greater joy than to hear that my children are walking in the truth* (3 John 4).

- Above all, the greatest need of those we are lifting in prayer is to love God and to enter a personal relationship with Him.[7]

For other ideas on praying specifically for others, see the Detailing Tools Section.

Our Encouragement

Whether grandparent, parent, friend, mentor, or other role, your regular interaction with and influence on the one you are praying for is more important than you might think. That person, no matter the age, is your priority for this season of your life.

God has ordained this season. He alone in His sovereignty determined that you would fulfill this role for this person, at this time. And He equips us for this calling through the power of His Holy Spirit within us and through Scripture. In the Bible we can find encouragement as we pray.

> "To the world you may be one person but to one person you may be the world."[8]
>
> (Anonymous)

Biblical Encouragements to Pray

- Pray with no doubt in your heart, believing what God says, and it will be done (Mark 11:23).

- Don't lose heart in praying (Luke 18:1-8).

- The Holy Spirit will assist you when you aren't sure how to pray (Romans 8:26).

- Always thank God for your loved one with real joy in your heart. Thank Him for each memory of them He has allowed you to have (Philippians 1:3-4).

- Do not be anxious about anything concerning the one for whom you are praying. Rather, *in everything by prayer and supplication with thanksgiving let your requests be made known to God* (Philippians 4:6).

- Don't give up. *Pray without ceasing* (1 Thessalonians 5:17).

- Your prayers for those you love have great power as they are working (James 5:16).

- Prayer should be our passion. We cannot control others. They will not always listen to our counsel and advice. They may seldom, if ever, write or call or visit, but God has orchestrated our relationship with them. They belong to us. May we never stop praying for them (1 Samuel 12:23).

- As you pray day after day, year after year, for those God has entrusted to you through a special relationship of some sort, know that your prayers are not in vain.

Pray-ers as Encouragers

Let those special persons know you are praying for them. That knowledge can be more powerful than even your presence. It can also serve as a valuable reminder that they are loved and they matter.

Be sure they know you are praying for them when they have a specific need or are struggling with a problem.

Recently, I was able to spend some time with my nine-year-old granddaughter. It was nearing the end of the school year, and she had many things going on—a speech meet, talent show, piano competition, and a piano recital. We discussed these events, and I shared with her that I was praying for her. After the speech meet, she called to let me know how it had gone. Before we hung up, I reminded her that I was praying for the upcoming piano competition. The night prior to the competition, my granddaughter had her mom send me a text to remind me of my commitment to pray for her.

Your prayers can serve to strengthen your relationship with the one for whom you pray. As you consistently live out a life of prayer, those special ones may become more inclined to share with you what they feel they can't share with anyone else.

If possible, let your loved ones see your Prayer Journal or Prayer Calendar. Share entries with them. If you Pray in Color (directions in the Shaping Tools Section) for those on your prayer list, mail the finished product to them. Tell them when and what you prayed for them, and if you have a regular prayer time for them, let them know when it is. Also, when that special person you have been praying for shares with you an answer to one of your prayers, be sure you give the Lord gratitude both privately and publicly for His graciousness. Gratitude is of great benefit to you and contagious to others.

As you are fulfilling your role of encourager to others, you will also encourage a sense of hope in them by modeling your trust in the Lord, even during uncertain times.

Dear Pray-er, remember this familiar quote, "To the world you may be one person but to one person you may be the world." (Anonymous)

Our Legacy

The greatest, lasting gift we can give to those we love is the gift of our time and prayers. We may not leave them monetary riches or an estate of great wealth, but we can leave them a clear example of persistent prayer, even in times of discouragement.

As we grow older, I think most of us begin to think about what kind of legacy we will leave. We want to feel that we made a difference. We want to be remembered. The most valuable legacy any of us can leave is a godly legacy. Our heart's desire should be that we are remembered as someone who loved God deeply and pointed others toward Him. May our legacy be that our loved ones know and remember His name—the Name worthy of being remembered.

One way each of us can leave a godly legacy is to be a prayerful follower of Christ. Yes, it's important to pray before meals, but it's also important to allow others to see us in prayer at other times: in church, attending prayer meetings, on our knees in our home. We can leave a legacy of prayer by sharing our prayer requests and prayer journals with our family members and friends. Regularly engaging in prayer for these same precious souls while in their presence is another way to leave a godly legacy of prayer. Face-to-face is a wonderful way to do this; however, if face-to-face prayer isn't possible, get creative. Pray together with others over the phone, FaceTime, or Skype. In addition to sharing your love of God and the importance of prayer in such ways, you will be creating an affirming experience for those you love. Can you imagine the boost children, or persons of any age for that matter, will receive, knowing and hearing that someone cares enough not only to pray for them, but also about things that are important to them?

> *One generation shall praise Your works to another, and shall declare Your mighty acts.*
>
> Psalm 145:4 (NKJV)

For those who may be praying for a special child in their life, I'd like to encourage you to incorporate the practice of praying together into your relationship with that child. Praying with children is a wonderful way to model personal conversation with God and to encourage children in the practice. As you begin to pray with them, don't underestimate the power of sharing your requests with children. Whether or not they choose to pray for you is their decision, but by asking for their prayers you imply several important lessons. First, you are communicating that even adults need prayers. Additionally, you are letting them know you are still growing in your spiritual life and you do not have all the answers. Entrusting the young ones in your life with your prayer requests conveys to them that the prayers of children are important and that we all need each other. And personally, there's the added boost the child will receive from feeling entrusted with the privilege of praying for an adult.

Be specific with your requests when sharing them with others, including children. This practice not only helps others better know how to pray for you, it also provides an excellent example for their own prayer life.

Scripture calls us to pray for the generations. It also calls us to be examples for them.

These words that I command you today shall be on your heart. You shall teach them diligently to your children, and shall talk of them when you sit in your house, and when you walk by the way, and when you lie down, and when you rise (Deuteronomy 6:6-7).

One generation shall commend your works to another, and shall declare your mighty acts (Psalm 145:4).

When we do things such as allowing our young family members to see us in prayer, sharing our prayer journals, and discussing prayer requests with them, we set an example of prayer. This is modeling. Another way we can model prayer for the generations is to stop and pray with them when we notice something we are particularly thankful for or to kneel and pray with them when they are nervous about an upcoming test or storm. Begin modeling when they are young, and it is likely they will practice what they have seen as they grow older.

We can also be examples of godly prayer to the children in our lives by joining their parents as they teach about praying. Teach the young that prayer is communication with God. It is asking Him to give us wisdom in the decisions we make in our daily lives, and it is talking over our problems with Him. Teach them most of all, that prayer is praising God for who He is and thanking Him for all the wonderful things He has done for us.

Children need to know that God is not a magic genie. They need to understand that prayer will not always change our circumstances. But they also need to know that prayer does change our attitude toward our circumstances when we recognize that the Lord is with us through the tough times as well as the easy times.

Impress upon their young hearts that God hears all our prayers, but He does not always answer them on our timetable. Share instances where God has said, "Yes," "No," and "Not yet." Share how He has been with you throughout your lifetime. You can have a part in helping the generations realize the power of prayer and that prayer is not all about them.

Another way to leave a godly legacy is to pray Scripture. What more effective way to thwart Satan's schemes and powers toward those you love than to pray His word, while at the same time unleashing the power and provision of God toward them?

In a discussion of prayer as it relates to our young family members, it is important to consider how prayer relates specifically to grandparents. It is through prayer that grandparents are called to preserve the treasures that exist in their families. *So even to old age and gray hairs, O God, do not forsake me, until I proclaim your might to another generation, your power to all those to come* (Psalm 71:18). The magnificent miracles of God, which result in answered prayers will, for all eternity, be a part of the legacy grandparents leave to their grandchildren. The prayers of grandparents make a difference. Through these prayers the faithfulness, sovereignty, and goodness of God are displayed to all the members of a family.

No matter where you are on life's journey, it's never too early to consider the legacy you will leave. May you become intentional about making it a legacy that points others to THE NAME, the only name worthy to be remembered.

Legacy Prayer

Heavenly Father, I ask that you give me your vision for the precious souls that I call family. Help me to make the commitment to pray consistently and specifically for each one. I pray for the strength and energy to stand firm in my commitment. Place others in my life who will hold me accountable to both the commitment and the follow through.

Lord, hear my prayers as I pray specifically for my family and others You place on my heart. Help me surrender my concerns to You and rest in the knowledge that You, O God, are sovereign. Accept my praises and thanksgiving as an offering of love and worship.

May I be intentional in caring for my own soul as well for I know that it is impossible to pour into others what I do not possess myself. Help me to be faithful to spend time in Your Word, for it's in these pages that I become versed in Your design and grow to know You better. Help me to become a wisdom hunter in the pages of Scripture. May I also be committed to times of personal prayer and self-reflection as care for my soul.

Help me to love my family well and to be a godly example for them. Help me to be faithful in my commitment to pray intentionally, consistently, and specifically. Help me to leave a legacy of faith.

Thank you for this precious gift of prayer. Amen.

Our Intention

Prayer is an aggressive, proactive work. It is an important work. Vital, in fact. In our role of pray-er, we can play a major part in stabilizing and influencing the lives of those we love.

With this ministry of prayer comes great responsibility. We must not take it lightly. Our resolve must be intentional about praying for others.

> "God shapes the world by prayer."[9]
> E. M. Bounds

Intention is an act of determination. We must be deliberate about being faithful in our prayers. Putting your precious loved ones on a calendar may seem cold or impersonal but doing so makes sure that prayer is not forgotten.

Secondly, our intentions must lead to result. Good intentions alone don't demonstrate our love, nor do they reflect the love of God. Good intentions with no follow through remain just that—good intentions.

We can all recall countless times when we have had good intentions, the best even, but nothing ever came of them. We've kicked ourselves, figuratively speaking, for letting our intentions remain just that. So how do we move from good intentions to an act carried through?

Begin by making the commitment, publicly. Write it out. Scribble it on an index card or use calligraphy on a sheet of beautiful stationery. Then place your written commitment in a highly visible spot. Tuck it in your Bible, stick it to your bathroom mirror, or hold it to the front of your refrigerator with cutesy little magnets. Afterward, share your commitment with someone. Enlist your spouse to make the commitment with you, profess your commitment to the one you are committing to pray for, or confess it to a close friend and have her hold you accountable.

Praying for others is a long-term commitment—one that we must take care not to enter lightly. Recall the battle (Ephesians 6:12). It is real. Satan is at work. He wants nothing more than our faith and the faith of our loved ones. We, dear pray-er, are fighting for souls! Please understand, the enemy cannot defeat our God; however, he can defeat a generation. The faith of our loved ones is his aim. They desperately need us to pray for them throughout the course of their lives—not just during a crisis.

To stay the course of this long-term commitment, we must persevere. Find ways to remind yourself to pray. It's so easy to get caught up in our day-to-day always thinking, "Just one more thing then I'll sit down to pray." Don't allow this to happen. Be intentional. Grab a calendar and write down what day you will pray for whom. Set the timer on your phone. When it goes off, stop what you are doing, and go pray.

Be consistent. Pray at the same time each day for the one you have designated. Set up a special, inviting "prayer" place. Go there and pray. It's one thing to make this long-term commitment for one soul. It's quite another to remain faithful in perseverance and consistency when the numbers grow larger. What if you are the grandparent of fifteen, the parent of four, or the teacher, coach, mentor, friend of twenty? My greatest piece of advice is to think ahead and keep things manageable. Grab your prayer calendar and set a schedule. Fifteen grandchildren? Choose the day of the week that works best for you, maybe Saturday morning. Designate that time for prayer. Then write in each grandchild's name. One a week for fifteen weeks. When you've reached the end of the fifteen weeks, simply repeat your schedule. Four children? Assign a day of the week for each child. Pray for the same child on the same day of each week. Twenty souls? Assign a day of the month for each one.

Will calendars and timers guarantee that we will pray for those we care deeply about with 100% consistency? Probably not, we are flawed, imperfect people, but calendars, timers, alarms, and thoughtful planning will certainly help us develop great habits and to be more consistent than we would be otherwise.

I must confess. This is me. Great intentions. Easily sidetracked. Always trying to get just one more thing accomplished before I do the truly important. These are my struggles. It is my responsibility to identify them and to own them. Rather than allowing my struggles to continue to be barriers to my prayers, it is imperative that I create intentional strategies that will enable me to go the distance in my long-term commitment of prayer.

Don't wait another day. It is all too easy to come to the end of a day without having spent any time in prayer for others. Our others need us. They need our prayers. Put your post in the ground for them today. Make your commitment public. Sit down with your daily schedule and your calendar. Devise strategies for the long haul and write them down. Give prayer proper priority in your life. Be intentional.

Our Call

Each of us is called to pray for others.

Pour out your heart like water before the presence of the Lord! Lift up your hands to him for the lives of your children (Lamentations 2:19).

[D]o not be anxious about anything, but in everything by prayer and supplication with thanksgiving let your requests be made known to God (Philippians 4:6).

The prayer of a righteous person is powerful and effective (James 5:16, NIV).

Like Queen Esther who stood in the gap for her people, the Jews, when Haman plotted to destroy them, I desire to stand in the gap for my "people." In this season of life, my "people" are my grandchildren, my children, and my husband. It may be the same for you, but quite possibly your "people" includes nieces, nephews, students, or co-workers.

No matter who your "people" are, be assured that Satan certainly does not want you to pray for them. He does not want any of us standing in the gap. He knows only too well that if the weakest saints get on their knees, he will be defeated in gaining the hearts and minds he so desperately seeks.

> *I searched for a man among them who would build up the wall and stand in the gap before Me for the land, so that I would not destroy it; but I found no one.*
>
> Ezekiel 22:30 (NASB)

This is our call. It is our time. Who will stand in the gap for our "people," their families, their schools, their workplace, their world, if not us?

James Dobson, founder of Focus on the Family, received this question from a listener who asked, "Okay, I understand the strong-willed child better than I did. But tell me how to get our son through these tough years. He is tough as nails. What specific suggestions do you have for us?" Dr. Dobson answered: "*We must bathe them in prayer every day of their lives. The God who made your children will hear your petitions. He has promised to do so. After all, He loves them more than you do.*"[10]

Don't allow the fear that you don't know what to pray for your loved ones or might not pray as eloquently as someone else hinder you from fulfilling this vital role. In Romans 8:26 Paul tells us that the Holy Spirit intercedes for us when we don't know what to pray. The Holy Spirit knows the needs of those you have committed to pray for. Ask Him to intercede according to His will. Put your burdens and requests in His hands and leave them there.

Blessed pray-er, consider it both an honor and a privilege to lift your precious ones to the Lord. There is no greater thing we can do to express love than to pray consistently for them.

May you know that God will answer even the most impossible requests if you will but ask Him.

PART 2

Shaping Tools

Many of us have been raised on traditional models when it comes to our prayer time—kneeling beside our bed, sitting in a chair in a quiet corner of our home, head bowed, and eyes closed. While there is certainly a time and place for these postures, some of us find that on occasion a different approach is needed.

It could be that our personality is simply not suited to absolute stillness and quiet, or perhaps there are times when we find our minds wandering and ourselves distracted, or maybe we just enjoy variety.

In this section, you will find several different models for your prayer time. The methods shared here include such things as writing, drawing, making calendars, and taking photos. Some offer help to those with wandering minds who are easily distracted. Some of the methods will speak to those who are artistic or visual. As you read through the prayer methods offered here, think about how God has wired you. Perhaps you can find a method or two that fits with your own personal God-wiring.

The ideas shared here are just a sampling of the many diverse ways you can engage in prayer. This list is certainly not exhaustive. If your wiring includes music, find a way to incorporate music into your prayers. Wired for dance? Then find a way to dance as you pray. Be creative. Have fun. Take any of these ideas and rework them to design a prayer method that is uniquely you or be inspired to invent a model that is completely your own.

The important thing is that you find a way (or multiple ways—mix them up) that will help draw you toward more intentional and consistent prayer for those you love.

Prayer Journal

There are several variations of the prayer journal. No matter which type of journal seems best fitted to you, it is important to remember that each of these journals is intended to be a working document, not a keepsake album. Choose the variation that seems "doable" for you or use the ideas to come up with a version all your own.

Picture Prayer Journal

A Picture Prayer Journal is a simple and effective prayer tool. Using a blank journal, spiral notebook, or stenographer's pad, set up a separate "info" page for each of the people on your prayer list. You might choose to create a Picture Prayer Journal for your children, grandchildren, Sunday school class, small group members, or any other group of people you pray for regularly.

When deciding on what type of book to use as your Picture Prayer Journal, consider when and where you will be using it. If it will be housed and used most in one location, you might choose a larger format book. If you prefer to carry it in your purse, computer bag, or Bible, the smaller sized stenographer's pad might be the best option.

As you plan the layout of your journal, consider leaving a blank page or two between each person's "info" page. This will help to keep the notebook from filling up so quickly and having to be replaced often.

To set up your journal, write the name of each person on your prayer list across the top of a page or in the top right-hand corner. Include their birthdate just below their name. In the upper left-hand corner, glue a small photo if you have one. Wallet-sized school photos work well for any children on your list, but any small photo will do.

Once your journal is ready to go, fill up its pages with notes and prayer requests specific to the individual. If you have trouble getting started, here are some basic needs:

- Health and safety—mental, physical, and spiritual
- Growth—physical, spiritual
- Peer pressure
- Strength to resist temptations from sex, drug abuse, the internet, etc.
- Godly character

- Spiritual walk

- Physical needs

- Be sure to include specific requests on each page. Be attentive each time you talk with someone who is part of your prayer journal. Listen closely. Hear their need. These might include:

- Making the team

- Landing the job

- Medical needs—injuries, illnesses, tests, procedures

- A solo performance

- Relationships

- Difficulties at work or school

- Grades, and more

One important and practical tip for making entries into your Picture Prayer Journal is to use a pencil. This will make it easier for you to update your journal or to make corrections.

Just as the format of your journal should be adjusted to meet your own style, so should the use of your journal. There are many options for putting your prayer journal into practice. As you determine how praying with your journal will work best for you, be sure to consider the number of people you have committed to pray for, the number of requests written in your journal, and your personal schedule. The idea is to be intentional and consistent in prayer. Use of your prayer journal should be scheduled; however, to keep it from becoming another "thing attempted but not carried through," try not to overcommit. Start small. You can always increase your use of the journal and your prayer time as this new habit is formed. Remember, praying for one person a day or assigning each person listed in your journal a specific day or week are manageable ways to help with perseverance and consistency with your commitment.

Pictorial Prayer Journal

In her book, *A Car Seat in My Convertible?*, Sharon Hoffman describes her Pictorial Prayer Journal.

> This prayer journal is housed in a loose-leaf, three-ring binder. The binder makes the journal simple and portable. The loose-leaf paper makes it easy to replace pages as needed. In this journal, photos are used as prayer prompts.
>
> The emphasis on photos might make this the journal of choice for those who are visually motivated. Rather than lengthy prayer lists, your journal will be full of photos of the people you have committed to pray for.
>
> As in the Picture Prayer Journal, a page is dedicated to each person; however, rather than just one small photo in the corner of the page, this journal is intended to be full of photos. After setting up the journal, you may even find yourself taking photos with the specific goal of adding them to your pages.[11]

In her description of the use of her journal, Hoffman shares that these "scrapbooked" pages enable her to focus so much better during her prayer time than she was able to with her old lists. She also states that while praying for each of her grandchildren, she likes to "hold their hand" by placing her hand on a crayon-traced handprint of the child's hand, which she has glued directly onto their individual page. This is a great idea for those of you who are tactile and praying for a special child in your life. I have a friend who meets her need for touch by wearing a charm bracelet when she prays. On her bracelet is a charm for each of her children and grandchildren. Touching the corresponding bead for each family member as she prays helps her stay focused.

To get started with your Pictorial Prayer Journal, grab a three-ring binder, some loose-leaf paper, and several photos of the people you wish to include in your journal. You will also need some glue or adhesive. Set up one page per person. Don't forget to leave some space for writing out your prayers if that is something you want to include. Another set-up option is to write in Scripture verses for each person as you glue in their photos. Choose verses that apply to the individual's specific needs and circumstances and personalize them by substituting names for pronouns.

As a grandmother, photographer, and keeper of memories, I love the idea of this Pictorial Prayer Journal. What a joy it will be many years from now to pull out journals filled to the brim with old photographs, prayers, verses, and memories.

The Pictorial Prayer Journal, like any of the prayer journals shared here, will become a record of God's faithfulness in the lives of your family and friends. Create your journal, set up your prayer schedule, and begin today.

Traditional Prayer Journal

If you've ever used a prayer journal, more likely than not, it was this one. All you need for a traditional prayer journal is some type of notebook or blank journal and your favorite writing instrument.

Different than the Picture Prayer Journal and the Pictorial Prayer Journal, this journal is sectioned off by categories. Consider including any of the following:

- Requests
- Prayers
- Praises
- Answers to Prayers
- Favorite Scriptures
- Favorite Quotes
- Photos
- Notes

Once your journal is set up and ready to go, use it during your prayer time. When making entries, be sure to begin each one by placing the date at the top of the page. You might also want to include the time and your location.

Develop your own system of filling in your categories and using what you have recorded as prompts for your prayers. Decide if you will write out your prayers each time you use your journal, occasionally, or not at all. Don't forget to record your praises or list things for which you are thankful each time you use your journal. Praise and thanks are good for the soul and help keep us focused on Jesus.

Another good habit to develop is to record answered prayers. In these entries, be sure to include the date and any details about how God worked in that specific situation.

Legacy Prayer Journal

Ready for something different? To this point, we've shared only prayer journaling methods intended for use by an individual. How about a prayer journal where you invite those you are praying for to participate with you in the journaling process? The legacy prayer journal was originally designed to be completed by two generations of a family: grandparents and grandchildren or all the generations of a family; however, it could also easily be used by members of a Sunday school class, team, or small group. This journal variation has multiple benefits. It creates community, builds relationships, and provides a wonderful opportunity for some one-on-one modeling of prayer.

The legacy journal is all about praying and sharing together. Therefore, as a group you will need to begin by deciding when and how you will best be able to use the journal. Keep in mind the various schedules represented and any geographical challenges that might exist. For instance, if all members of the journaling group live in the same area and meet regularly on Thursdays, plan to make your entries at the beginning of your weekly meeting. If your grandchildren or other family members live miles away, however, your plan will need to take that into consideration. For instance, you might decide to make the entries by Skype or video chat each Tuesday and make face-to-face entries during visits together. Keep in mind that there are no hard and fast rules in setting up your plan. It is a matter of choosing to implement a prayer plan and then adjusting it to meet your needs.

Once you have a plan for using your legacy journal, it's time to gather supplies and start putting your journal together. You will need a journal that can be divided into sections or a three-ring binder, loose-leaf paper, and section dividers. If children are a part of your group, consider letting them help decorate the cover. They could use family photos, pictures from magazines, or they can draw something of their own.

Next, set up the inside of your journal. Possible section ideas include: prayer requests, prayers, praises, and answers to prayer.

Once the journal is set up and ready to go, begin recording entries at the predetermined place and time. Be sure all members of the group have an opportunity to record their entries.

Periodically, it is good to observe a "share time." One plan is to designate a time when entries are read aloud to one another. Another option is to include a section in the back of your journal for summaries. Then each week or once a month have one of the journal contributors write a one or two sentence summary of the entries made during that period. If this option is chosen, summaries should be shared with the other contributors.

No matter your choice of style, prayer journals are a powerful tool in carrying out your role of pray-er. Both the journaling process and the journal itself reap huge benefits to the ones you are praying for and to you. Journaling your prayers benefits others because the journals serve to remind you, their prayer warrior, to regularly pray. Additionally, if you choose to share your journal with the ones you are praying for, they benefit from the dialogue and modeling of prayer. Journaling benefits you, the pray-er, in several ways. First, the act of writing is good for you. There is actual science that backs up the power that writing has on the brain. The act of writing also helps you stay focused during your prayer time with God. Recording your prayers also allows you to take a closer look at what is happening in your own mind and heart and will help your personal relationship with God grow deeper. Completed journals are a beautiful visual reminder to you and to your loved ones of God's faithfulness and His continued presence in their lives.

Praying in Color

A few years ago, I found this tool that is now one of my all-time favorites. During the sharing of her story with a group of gathered women, my pastor's wife mentioned something called "praying in color." I became curious—curious enough to attend a workshop she gave on the topic the following spring. Describing herself as "most comfortable with art supplies in her hands and ballet slippers on her feet," she stated that discovering this concept set her free. Until praying in color, my pastor's wife said that like many of us, she had spent years struggling in her prayer and devotion life.

Praying in color is based on the book of the same name written by Sybil MacBeth. The basic concept of praying in color is to keep your pencil moving while you commune with God. This, for many, provides focus and keeps the mind from wandering or going blank.

During the workshop presentation, we practiced praying in color together in the form of intercessory prayer. In her book, Sybil MacBeth offers other ideas for praying in color such as using the time to pray the names of God, to have a conversation with God, or to pray the Scriptures.[12]

In the days following the workshop, I considered praying in color and how I might use it to pray for my grandchildren. This process has without a doubt become one of the most powerful prayer tools in my toolbox.

I decided first that I would pray in color for each of my grandchildren. At that time, we had eight grandchildren. To make it manageable, I decided I would pray for a different child each Monday. I decided that I would also like to use this "Monday time" to pray Scripture for my grandchildren.

On the first Monday, I sat down with a sheet of drawing paper and some colored pencils. I began by writing my grandchild's name in the center of the paper. Then as I concentrated my prayer specifically on her, I kept the pencils moving by embellishing her written name—adding design, doodles, and color. My prayer as I doodled her name was one of thanks to God for her, gratitude for the treasure she is to our family, and for her future. I spent two to three minutes on this opening portion of my prayer.

I then spent the remainder of my prayer time praying Scripture for my granddaughter. To keep things moving, I used the "Scriptures to Pray for Your Grandchildren" resource which can be found in the Detailing Tools Section of this book. Allowing the Holy Spirit to lead me, I selected a Scripture to pray, wrote it on the paper, and embellished it—again, adding things like design, doodles, words, phrases, and color as I prayed. I continued in this manner until I felt it was time to close the prayer. When my prayer ended, I had prayed six Scriptures from the resource for my granddaughter. I have prayed in this manner for my grandchildren several times now and find that typically I will pray anywhere from about five to ten Scriptures during a prayer.

Once I finished the "process" of prayer, I hung my prayer (the product) on the front of our refrigerator as a reminder to my husband and me to pray for our granddaughter throughout the day. The following day, I took the prayer down, folded it up, and mailed it to her, along with a personal note, letting her know that I had prayed specifically for her. I have now mailed several prayers to my grandchildren and find that the prayers become treasured keepsakes. I've spotted them folded up in the back of a Bible, hung on bulletin boards, under pillows, and in "treasure" drawers.

My grandchildren now range in age from two to 13 years old. For the older grandchildren, I generally include the Scripture references on their praying in color pages. For the younger children, I try to keep the use of words to a minimum. I often use drawings and symbols on their prayers with maybe a single word from the Scripture I pray for them. An alternative resource to use when praying for children is the "Suggestions to Pray for Different Stages of Life" which is also included in the Detailing Tools Section.

Grandparents often get caught up in the "I can't draw" syndrome or the "What are the rules?" mentality. It's important to know that you don't have to be an artist to pray in color. I've included a few prayer art ideas to give you an idea. It's also essential to know that there are NO rules when it comes to praying in color. I gave a demonstration of praying in color to the women of my small group a few months ago, and while we all participated in the same activity, none of the five prayers looked anything alike.

Praying in color can be engaged individually or as a corporate act of prayer. Gather a group of friends and pray in color together for your spouse, your children, your grandchildren, or a missionary family. Pray corporately with the children you are praying for. When your grandchildren are visiting or after the family has finished dinner, gather the group together around a table filled with drawing paper and coloring supplies.

If this is a first experience with praying in color for your gathered group of children, be sure to explain the process to them in age-appropriate language before you begin. Then together decide who each of you will be praying for.

Praying in color with children is an excellent way to model prayer. It is also a wonderful demonstration of how more than one person can be "talking" to God at the same time, and your individual coloring pages will give you much to talk about once all have finished with their prayers.

Prayer Art Ideas For Praying in Color

- Lines (spirals, zigzags, wavy, arcs, etc.)
- Shapes (circles, squares, triangles, rectangels, elipses, polygons, clouds, dots, etc.)

Monthly Prayer Calendars

Monthly prayer calendars are another way to establish an effective prayer ministry.

You will need an inexpensive yearly, month-by-month calendar. You might want to consider purchasing one that is small enough to fit into your purse or Bible so that you have constant easy access to it.

At the beginning of each new year, write in the birthdays of each person you are committing to pray for in the coming year. Then, as you learn of special events or happenings in their lives, add the dates to your calendar. These notations serve as prayer reminders and prompts for praying specifically. Examples of marked dates may include birthdays, weddings, graduations, exams, tests, recitals, team try-outs, getting braces off, and baptisms. You will not necessarily be informed of every event in the lives of those you are praying for, but by developing the habit of listening with purpose you will be able to pick up on many.

As with all the prayer tools in this section, monthly prayer calendars can be adapted to fit your own style and personality. Below are some suggestions for other ways to use the monthly prayer calendar:

- Use the "Scriptures to Pray for Your Children" (see page 90) resource to pray each Scripture once a day for a month.

- Pray Scriptures of praise to the Lord each day for a month using the "Scripture Praise" resource (see page 76).

- Guide your prayers for one month using "65 Specific Prayers for Your Husband" (see page 52).

- For concentrated prayer, use the "12 Ways to Pray for Your Child's Future Mate" and pray one item from the list for a month before moving to the next (see page 62).

- If you prefer not to pray one Scripture, goal, or virtue per day, you might choose to pray one per week.

In whatever way you decide to set up your prayer calendar, make it a habit. Refer to your calendar each day. Then pray.

Praying Scripture

One beautiful way to pray for others is to pray Scripture for them. To personalize your Scripture prayers, insert the name of the one you are praying for into the Scriptures as you pray.

If you are struggling to know exactly where to begin or what Scriptures to use, here are some suggestions to help you get started:

Prayer Guides

There are several prayer guides located in the Detailing Tools Section of this book. While all of them are Scripture-based, the following guides lend themselves specifically to the praying of Scriptures:

- Scriptures to Pray for Godly Character
- Scriptures to Pray for Your Children
- 12 Ways to Pray for Your Child's Future Mate
- Scriptures to Pray for Grandchildren
- 65 Specific Prayers for Your Husband
- Praying Scripture for Your Marriage
- Scripture Praise
- Praying Scripture for Singles
- Scriptures to Pray in a Season of Waiting
- Scriptures to Pray for My Wife
- Scriptures to Pray for Yourself

If you have never prayed Scriptures before, these guides might be a good place to begin.

Pray Passages

Another way to pray Scripture for others is to identify appropriate Scripture passages and pray them, inserting the names of the individuals you are praying for. Below are some wonderful passages to use:

- The Prayers of Paul: Ephesians 1:15-23; Ephesians 3:14-21; Philippians 1:9-11; Colossians 1:9-12

- Aaron's Priestly Blessing: Numbers 6:22-27

- Many of the Psalms, especially Psalm 91 and Psalm 139, are good places to begin

- The Book of Proverbs

Pray any of these Scripture passages. Simply insert an individual's name into the verses of the passage or express the principles or ideas from the passage as a prayer.

Prayer Box

There are countless ways to use a Prayer Box. You might choose to implement one of the options shared here or decide to put your own spin on one, creating something uniquely you.

Option 1—Journal in a Box

When using this type of prayer box, your prayer requests are simply written on slips of paper and placed into the box rather than written in a journal. The physical placement of each request into the box can be a symbol of letting go and giving the request to God. In fact, some find it helpful to consciously do just that as they place their requests into the box.

The prayer box itself can be anything: store bought or handmade, elaborate or simple, large or small. If you prefer to purchase a prayer box, a quick Internet search will turn up a wide variety of options. For the do-it-yourselfer, prayer boxes can be made of cardboard boxes, shoe boxes, plastic containers, glass jars, coffee cans, or just about anything else that has been emptied.

It is best to determine a time frame for the use of your prayer box. You might decide to keep it for one month, three months, six months, or a year.

At the end of the predetermined time, you have the choice to do whatever you wish with your prayer box and its contents. Read through the requests within your box and then store the box away as a chronicle and testimony for family members. Ceremoniously burn the requests in your fireplace, throw them in the trash, or come up with something all your own.

Option 2—Symbolic Box

For this prayer box option, small objects such as colored stones represent your prayer requests.

The actual prayer box and its use are the same as Journal in a Box (Option 1), except that instead of writing out your prayer requests on slips of paper, a stone representing your request is placed into your box.

Bags of small colored stones can be purchased online or at any craft store. The stones represent requests or other things for which you are praying, and they serve as a visual reminder. Again, it can be helpful to consciously visualize letting go of each request or problem and giving it to the Lord as stones are placed into the box.

To add to the visual impact, another small object can be chosen to represent praises or answers to prayers. These objects can also be placed in the box as a visual representation of giving praise and thanks to the Lord.

No matter the type of prayer box you use, there is flexibility. Prayer boxes can be kept for requests, thanksgiving, praise, self-reflection, or anything else you need to take to the Lord in prayer. Prayer boxes can also be kept individually or by a family or group of people who pray together. In this case, all the members of the group become contributors.

Including children in a group prayer box is a great way of modeling and teaching prayer. It helps them learn to turn to God, rely on Him, and express their gratitude. Inclusion in the process also draws children into "prayer" conversations.

When keeping a group prayer box, periodic times of sharing can be incorporated. During sharing time, individuals can share publicly about some of the requests and praises they have committed to God. Sharing time, however, should always begin with a reminder to share only those things each person is comfortable with sharing—it is always voluntary, and privacy is to be respected.

Prayer Log

A prayer log is very similar to the traditional prayer journal listed previously; however, a prayer log can be even more streamlined. Simply keep a running list of prayer requests and/or answers to prayer as you receive them.

One thing I have found helpful when keeping a prayer log is to use different colors of ink for the entries. Use one color for requests and another for answers.

To encourage intergenerational dialogue about prayer, suggest that your children, grandchildren, or any members of a cross-generational group keep a personal prayer log. Then provide times for sharing.

Pray Continually: 15 Ways to Practice 1 Thessalonians 5:17

In 1 Thessalonians 5:17 we find the command to *pray continually*. That means we should pray ALL THE TIME! Here are some ideas from Cheri Gamble's blog post of the same name to help you put this principle into practice. Use ideas from this list as you pray for and with others. Prayer is powerful—even if the prayer takes place in a car at a stoplight!

Passing-By Prayers

Also known as "drive-by prayers," this simply means that you get in a car and go for a drive, praying for the people and places you see as you drive by. You can plan a route or make it random.

Red Light Prayers

The next time you are stopped at a red light, spend time praying for the person in the car beside you, behind you, or anywhere else near you. If there are no vehicles near you, pray for the nearby businesses.

Ambulance Prayers

The next time you hear an ambulance or fire truck—stop, drop, and PRAY! Every siren you hear means someone, somewhere is in trouble, and could use your prayers!

Yuletide Prayers

Save all the Christmas cards you receive, shuffle them, and draw out one each day. In the new year, pray for the family that sent the card. With the reduced number of Christmas cards being mailed out in recent years, you may have to adapt this to drawing one out each week or each month.

Church Directory Prayers

If your church has a church directory, get it out and pray for each of the families that are represented in it. This also enables one to become more familiar with the members of your church! If you attend a large church, take a page a day.

On the Spot Prayer

The next time someone asks you to pray for him, stop what you are doing and pray right then and there. This is much more effective than saying you will pray later and then forgetting all about it.

Neighborhood Prayers

Take a stroll around your neighborhood and pray for the people who live in each of the houses. Do this on a regular basis and you may make some new friends in the process!

Thankfulness Chain

Leading up to Thanksgiving, make a paper chain. Have each of your family members write one thing they are thankful for on a piece of paper each day for a specified period of time. Gather the papers and assemble the chain. On Thanksgiving Day, take the chain down and pray, thanking God for each of the items.

International Prayer Focus

Choose a country and make a prayer calendar listing a different item to pray for each day. Visit The Voice of the Martyrs at https://www.persecution.com/ or Kids of Courage at http://www.kidsofcourage.com for some ideas and prayer suggestions!

Newspaper Prayers

Get out the newspaper (or check the Internet) and spend time in prayer for the items found in the headlines that day.

Utilize a Prayer Basket

At the beginning of each month, write peoples' names down on separate pieces of paper and place them in a basket. Then, draw a name out each day and pray for that person.

At the Store Prayers

The next time you are grocery shopping, pray for the people you pass in the aisles. After you leave, pray for the cashier who checked you out.

Lunch Box Prayers

Pray for your children, grandchildren, or husband as you pack their lunch. Then write a note and stick it in the lunch box, letting them know that you prayed.

Laundry Mat Prayers

The next time you are folding laundry pray for the person who owns the item you are folding. Go one step further and pray for the situations he will encounter the next time he is wearing that item!

Yearbook Prayers

Take current or old yearbooks (or scrapbooks) and pray for the people you see on each page. This could also be turned into "Facebook prayers," where you go through your friends' list, praying for each person you see.[14]

Pray without ceasing, continually, all the time, every single chance you have! God can do mighty things when His people pray!

PART 3

Almighty God,

we entrust all who are dear to us

to thy never-failing care and love,

for this life and the life to come;

knowing that thou art doing for them

better things than we can desire or pray for;

through Jesus Christ our Lord.[15]

Amen.

Detailing Tools

In this section are several prayer guides—guides meant to help you pray more specifically for others and yourself. It is my hope that you will find one or more resources that will enable you to more quickly and easily live out your God-created design as a pray-er for others.

Many of the prayer resources in this section are specific to a role or relationship. Others are geared toward a life season or topic. Among the guides you will find some that support the praying of Scripture. There are others that offer detailed ideas for things to pray. Whatever your preference, both formats offer many suggestions for the one who desires to pray more specifically.

Remember that the guides are just that, guides. Select a guide and pray each item from beginning to end. Pray only the things from the guide that the Holy Spirit prompts you to, or utilize the guide to help you pray, using one of the prayer models from Section Two. For example, I frequently use "Scriptures to Pray for Grandchildren" while Praying in Color. Another idea is to select a guide and pray through it in a month.

Please keep in mind that these prayer resources are provided as tools to get you started on your prayer journey. Use one or more of them. Use parts of some. Use them for other roles. Perhaps you will want to use Scriptures to Pray for Yourself as your pray for your pastor's wife. But don't use any of them blindly. Always rely on the Holy Spirit's guidance and the Holy Scriptures before using any part of the included resources. If you are not personally comfortable with any of the resources or any parts of them, do not use them. They are here as a help. Make them work for you.

It is my prayer that these resources will help move your prayers from vague to victorious.

65 Specific Prayers for Your Husband

Pray that your husband will…

Be Holy - [B]ut as he who called you is holy, you also be holy in all your conduct, since it is written, "You shall be holy, for I am holy" (1 Peter 1:15-16).

Seek the Lord with His Whole Heart - Blessed are those whose way is blameless, who walk in the law of the Lord! Blessed are those who keep his testimonies, who seek him with their whole heart (Psalm 119:1-2).

Grow Spiritually - But grow in the grace and knowledge of our Lord and Savior Jesus Christ. To him be the glory both now and to the day of eternity. Amen (2 Peter 3:18).

Love God with His Entire Being - You shall love the Lord your God with all your heart and with all your soul and with all your might (Deuteronomy 6:5).

Love Others with Biblical Love - Love is patient and kind; love does not envy or boast; it is not arrogant or rude. It does not insist on its own way; it is not irritable or resentful; it does not rejoice at wrongdoing, but rejoices with the truth. Love bears all things, believes all things, hopes all things, endures all things (1 Corinthians 13:4-7).

Fear the Lord - Praise the Lord! Blessed is the man who fears the Lord, who greatly delights in his commandments! (Psalm 112:1).

Have a Sincere and Genuine Faith - The aim of our charge is love that issues from a pure heart and a good conscience and a sincere faith (1 Timothy 1:5).

Hunger and Thirst for God - As a deer pants for flowing streams, so pants my soul for you, O God. My soul thirsts for God, for the living God. When shall I come and appear before God? (Psalm 42:1-2).

Guard His Heart - Keep your heart with all vigilance, for from it flow the springs of life (Proverbs 4:23).

Walk Humbly with God - He has told you, O man, what is good; and what does the Lord require of you but to do justice, and to love kindness, and to walk humbly with your God? (Micah 6:8).

Serve God as His First Priority in Life - If then you have been raised with Christ, seek the things that are above, where Christ is, seated at the right hand of God (Colossians 3:1).

Grow in Wisdom - The beginning of wisdom is this: Get wisdom, and whatever you get, get insight (Proverbs 4:7).

Have a Heart of Gratitude - *I will bless the LORD at all times; his praise shall continually be in my mouth* (Psalm 34:1).

Be a Man of Prayer - *[P]ray without ceasing* (1 Thessalonians 5:17).

Walk in Integrity - *The righteous who walks in his integrity—blessed are his children after him!* (Proverbs 20:7).

See His Sin as God Does - *Wash me thoroughly from my iniquity, and cleanse me from my sin! For I know my transgressions, and my sin is ever before me. Against you, you only, have I sinned and done what is evil in your sight, so that you may be justified in your words and blameless in your judgment* (Psalm 51:2-4).

Learn to Take Every Thought Captive - *For the weapons of our warfare are not of the flesh but have divine power to destroy strongholds. We destroy arguments and every lofty opinion raised against the knowledge of God, and take every thought captive to obey Christ* (2 Corinthians 10:4-5).

Draw Near to God - *Draw near to God, and he will draw near to you. Cleanse your hands, you sinners, and purify your hearts, you double-minded* (James 4:8).

Be Obedient to the Will of God - *But be doers of the word, and not hearers only, deceiving yourselves. For if anyone is a hearer of the word and not a doer, he is like a man who looks intently at his natural face in a mirror. For he looks at himself and goes away and at once forgets what he was like* (James 1:22-24).

Love Righteousness and Hate Wickedness - *The prudent sees danger and hides himself, but the simple go on and suffer for it* (Proverbs 27:12).

Recognize and Avoid Wickedness in Hs Own Life - *Therefore let anyone who thinks that he stands take heed lest he fall. No temptation has overtaken you that is not common to man. God is faithful, and he will not let you be tempted beyond your ability, but with the temptation he will also provide the way of escape, that you may be able to endure it* (1 Corinthians 10:12-13).

Run to God in Times of Trouble - *He who dwells in the shelter of the Most High will abide in the shadow of the Almighty. I will say to the LORD, "My refuge and my fortress, my God, in whom I trust"* (Psalm 91:1-2).

Be Protected by the Lord - *Guarding the paths of justice and watching over the way of his saints* (Proverbs 2:8).

Grow Daily in Character - *For this very reason, make every effort to supplement your faith with virtue, and virtue with knowledge, and knowledge with self-control, and self-control with steadfastness, and steadfastness with godliness, and godliness with brotherly affection, and brotherly affection with love. For if these qualities are yours and are increasing, they keep you from being ineffective or unfruitful in the knowledge of our Lord Jesus Christ* (2 Peter 1:5-8).

Learn to Be Content with Little or with Much - *[F]or we brought nothing into the world, and we cannot take anything out of the world. But if we have food and clothing, with these we will be content* (1 Timothy 6:7-8).

Have a Clear Conscience - *[H]aving a good conscience, so that, when you are slandered, those who revile your good behavior in Christ may be put to shame. For it is better to suffer for doing good, if that should be God's will, than for doing evil* (1 Peter 3:16-17).

Have Much Patience - *I therefore, a prisoner for the Lord, urge you to walk in a manner worthy of the calling to which you have been called, with all humility and gentleness, with patience, bearing with one another in love, eager to maintain the unity of the Spirit in the bond of peace* (Ephesians 4:1-3).

Stand Strong against Satan's Schemes - *Finally, be strong in the Lord and in the strength of his might. Put on the whole armor of God, that you may be able to stand against the schemes of the devil. For we do not wrestle against flesh and blood, but against the rulers, against the authorities, against the cosmic powers over this present darkness, against the spiritual forces of evil in the heavenly places* (Ephesians 6:10-12).

Be a Man of Courage - *Be strong and courageous. Do not fear or be in dread of them, for it is the Lord your God who goes with you. He will not leave you or forsake you* (Deuteronomy 31:6).

Be Faithful to His Wedding Vows - *Therefore a man shall leave his father and his mother and hold fast to his wife, and they shall become one flesh* (Genesis 2:24).

Love You as Christ Loved the Church - *Husbands, love your wives, as Christ loved the church and gave himself up for her, that he might sanctify her, having cleansed her by the washing of water with the word, so that he might present the church to himself in splendor, without spot or wrinkle or any such thing, that she might be holy and without blemish. In the same way husbands should love their wives as their own bodies. He who loves his wife loves himself. For no one ever hated his own flesh, but nourishes and cherishes it, just as Christ does the church* (Ephesians 5:25-29).

Protect His Heart against Inappropriate Relationships with the Opposite Sex - *For the commandment is a lamp and the teaching a light, and the reproofs of discipline are the way of life, to preserve you from the evil woman, from the smooth tongue of the adulteress* (Proverbs 6:23-24).

Be Always Captivated by Your Love - *Let your fountain be blessed, and rejoice in the wife of your youth, a lovely deer, a graceful doe. Let her breasts fill you at all times with delight; be intoxicated always in her love* (Proverbs 5:18-19).

Have a Pure and Undivided Heart in His Commitment to You - *But put on the Lord Jesus Christ, and make no provision for the flesh, to gratify its desires* (Romans 13:14).

Be Self-Controlled in Every Area of His Life - *For this very reason, make every effort to supplement your faith with virtue, and virtue with knowledge, and knowledge with self-control, and self-control with steadfastness, and steadfastness with godliness, and godliness with brotherly affection, and brotherly affection with love. For if these qualities are yours and are increasing, they keep you from being ineffective or unfruitful in the knowledge of our Lord Jesus Christ* (2 Peter 1:5-8).

Guide and Nurture the Growth of His Children - *Train up a child in the way he should go; even when he is old he will not depart from it* (Proverbs 22:6).

Take Responsibility for His Family's Spiritual Growth - *Hear, my son, and accept my words, that the years of your life may be many. I have taught you the way of wisdom; I have led you in the paths of uprightness. When you walk, your step will not be hampered, and if you run, you will not stumble. Keep hold of instruction; do not let go; guard her, for she is your life. Do not enter the path of the wicked, and do not walk in the way of the evil* (Proverbs 4:10-14).

Have the Wisdom to Lead His Family Physically, Emotionally, Mentally, and Spiritually - *The God of our Lord Jesus Christ, the Father of glory, may give you the Spirit of wisdom and of revelation in the knowledge of him, having the eyes of your hearts enlightened, that you may know what is the hope to which he has called you, what are the riches of his glorious inheritance in the saints, and what is the immeasurable greatness of his power toward us who believe, according to the working of his great might* (Ephesians 1:17-19).

Learn to Manage His Time Well - *Look carefully then how you walk, not as unwise but as wise, making the best use of the time, because the days are evil* (Ephesians 5:15-16).

Receive New Strength in Times of Busy Schedule - *They who wait for the Lord shall renew their strength; they shall mount up with wings like eagles; they shall run and not be weary; they shall walk and not faint* (Isaiah 40:31).

Increasingly Exhibit the Fruit of the Spirit - *But the fruit of the Spirit is love, joy, peace, patience, kindness, goodness, faithfulness, gentleness, self-control; against such things there is no law* (Galatians 5:22-23).

Work Hard to Provide for His Family - *Do not be slothful in zeal, be fervent in spirit, serve the Lord* (Romans 12:11).

Resist Satan - *Submit yourselves therefore to God. Resist the devil, and he will flee from you* (James 4:7).

Be Free from Stress - *And the peace of God, which surpasses all understanding, will guard your hearts and your minds in Christ Jesus* (Philippians 4:7).

Testify of His Faith to Others - *And he said to them, "Go into all the world and proclaim the gospel to the whole creation"* (Mark 16:15).

Build Godly Relationships with Other Believers - *And let us consider how to stir up one another to love and good works, not neglecting to meet together, as is the habit of some, but encouraging one another, and all the more as you see the Day drawing near* (Hebrews 10:24-25).

Practice Jesus-modeled Servant Leadership - *[Jesus] rose from supper. He laid aside his outer garments, and taking a towel, tied it around his waist. Then he poured water into a basin and began to wash the disciples' feet and to wipe them with the towel that was wrapped around him* (John 13:4-5).

Have Compassion for the World Around Him - *Put on then, as God's chosen ones, holy and beloved, compassionate hearts, kindness, humility, meekness, and patience, bearing with one another and, if one has a complaint against another, forgiving each other; as the Lord has forgiven you, so you also must forgive. And above all these put on love, which binds everything together in perfect harmony* (Colossians 3:12-14).

Have a Burden for Lost Souls - *"Go therefore and make disciples of all nations, baptizing them in the name of the Father and of the Son and of the Holy Spirit, teaching them to observe all that I have commanded you. And behold, I am with you always, to the end of the age"* (Matthew 28:19-20).

Listen to God and Desire to do His Will - *Not by the way of eye-service, as people-pleasers, but as bondservants of Christ, doing the will of God from the heart* (Ephesians 6:6).

Serve Unselfishly - *Do nothing from selfish ambition or conceit, but in humility count others more significant than yourselves. Let each of you look not only to his own interests, but also to the interests of others* (Philippians 2:3-4).

Speak Words That Build Up You and Your Family - *Let no corrupting talk come out of your mouths, but only such as is good for building up, as fits the occasion, that it may give grace to those who hear (Ephesians 4:29).*

Choose His Friends Wisely - *Whoever walks with the wise becomes wise, but the companion of fools will suffer harm (Proverbs 13:20).*

Have Men in His Life Who Will Encourage Him and Hold Him Accountable - *Iron sharpens iron, and one man sharpens another (Proverbs 27:17).*

Experience Physical, Emotional, Mental, Social, and Spiritual Strength - *That according to the riches of his glory he may grant you to be strengthened with power through his Spirit in your inner being (Ephesians 3:16).*

Live with an Eternal Perspective - *But seek first the kingdom of God and his righteousness, and all these things will be added to you (Matthew 6:33).*

Practice Forgiveness in All of His Relationships - *Be kind to one another, tenderhearted, forgiving one another, as God in Christ forgave you (Ephesians 4:32).*

Discipline His Children Wisely - *Fathers, do not provoke your children to anger, but bring them up in the discipline and instruction of the Lord (Ephesians 6:4).*

Mentor Younger Men - *You then, my child, be strengthened by the grace that is in Christ Jesus, and what you have heard from me in the presence of many witnesses entrust to faithful men, who will be able to teach others also (2 Timothy 2:1-2).*

Be Favored by God and Man - *And Jesus increased in wisdom and in stature and in favor with God and man (Luke 2:52).*

Discover and Live His God-given Purpose - *For I know the plans I have for you, declares the LORD, plans for welfare and not for evil, to give you a future and a hope (Jeremiah 29:11).*

Bring God Glory in Everything He Does - *So, whether you eat or drink, or whatever you do, do all to the glory of God (1 Corinthians 10:31).*

Understand the Importance of Taking Care of His Body - *Or do you not know that your body is a temple of the Holy Spirit within you, whom you have from God? You are not your own, for you were bought with a price. So glorify God in your body (1 Corinthians 6:19-20).*

Serve God and Others with Pure Motives - *Whatever you do, work heartily, as for the Lord and not for men, knowing that from the Lord you will receive the inheritance as your reward. You are serving the Lord Christ (Colossians 3:23-24).*

Praying for Your Children's/Grandchildren's Future

- Walk with God.
- Care of soul.
- Strength to stand.
- Protection from the enemy.
- Exhibit fruit of the Spirit.
- Live with an eternal perspective.
- Spiritual gifts.
- Talents.
- Purity of heart and mind.
- Find their identity in Christ.
- A passion for the things of God.
- Short-term and long-term goals.
- Godly spouse.
- Marriage based on biblical principles.
- Steady employment.
- Wise stewards of their resources.
- Parent their children with grace and wisdom.
- Children that love the Lord and follow His ways.
- Relationships within their family.
- Commitment to and follow-through of responsibilities.
- Wholesome forms of recreation.
- A heart of service to others.
- Qualities of leadership.
- Encouragement to others.
- Biblical time management.
- Kingdom building ministry.
- Care for aging parents.

Suggestions to Pray for Different Stages of Life

For Infants
- Develop a strong sense of security as they bond with their family.
- Feel safe and secure in their surroundings.
- Grow physically strong and mentally alert.
- Begin to lay a healthy foundation for good communication.
- Begin to develop a healthy attachment to their family members.

For Toddlers, pray they will:
- Develop a healthy self-image.
- Develop a sense of independence.
- Develop a sense of obedience to their parents.
- Be willing to try new, unfamiliar experiences.
- Feel secure apart from parents (i.e., with caregivers).
- Learn to play independently.

For Preschool age, pray they will:
- Develop a well-balanced personality.
- Learn problem resolution skills.
- Play well with others.
- Learn to obey quickly, and to respect authority.
- Explore and create without fear of failure.
- Develop a soft heart towards Jesus.
- Develop confidence and independence.
- Learn to control their emotions and anger.
- Develop an awareness of God's love for them.
- Build positive friendships.

For Elementary age, pray they will:

- Discover their God-given gifts and talents.
- Develop a sense of satisfaction and enjoyment using their skills.
- Be motivated, disciplined, and challenged in their learning experiences.
- Treat others with respect.
- Stand firm for what is right and refuse the wrong with a positive attitude.
- Choose friendships wisely.
- Obey their parents.
- Understand their need for a personal relationship with Jesus Christ.
- Develop a healthy self-confidence.
- Have a safe, healthy classroom environment.
- Be protected from the deception of the enemy.
- Develop a hunger for God's Word.

For Teenagers, pray they will:

- Be motivated, disciplined, and challenged to apply themselves and excel in their academic studies.
- Experience the reality of Jesus Christ in their lives, as they grow strong in their faith.
- Recognize the deception of the world.
- Be covered with God's safe keeping physically, spiritually, and emotionally.
- Date wisely (which leads to a spouse for a lifetime).
- Be sexually pure.
- Have open communication and a good relationship with parents.
- Choose friends who will have a positive influence.
- Grow spiritually with a hunger for God's Word.
- Have a balanced view of their beauty, charm, and strength.

For College/Young Adults, pray they will:

- Be motivated, disciplined and challenged to apply themselves in their studies to excel academically if they are in college.
- Seek God's wisdom and direction in their management of time, money, and talents.
- Think creatively and live with integrity.
- Recognize their gifts so they can find their God-given assignment.
- Provide the resources to fulfill their God-given assignment.
- Find a spouse who has a growing relationship with Jesus Christ.
- Be sexually pure.
- Be willing to accept responsibility and make wise financial decisions.
- Have open communication and a good relationship with parents.

For Those Married, pray they will:

- Understand how incredibly great God's power is to help if they ask Him.
- Establish spiritual disciplines as part of their lives.
- Read God's Word and pray together regularly as a couple.
- Seek God's guidance in the management of their time, money, and careers.
- Develop open and honest communication with their spouse.
- Grasp the importance of saying, "I'm sorry" and "I forgive you."
- Understand there is no such thing as too many hugs.
- Honor their parents.
- Be united in spirit and intent on one purpose.
- Be able to firmly stand against anything that might threaten their marriage.
- Be able to establish a stable, loving Christian home for their family.
- Recognize the deception and peer pressure of the world.[16]

12 Ways to Pray for Your Child's Future Mate

- Help my child's spouse to remain a virgin. Guard him from "outer-course" (petting experiences); abuse; harassment; and pornographic content in music, photographs, and movies. (See Colossians 3:5.)

- Make my child's spouse a man after God's own heart, a maturing Christian who will take a spiritual leadership role that encourages my daughter toward deeper spiritual growth. (See Ephesians 5:25–28.)

- Develop in my child's mate a desire to seek and ask forgiveness when wrong, from both God and man. (See 1 John 1:8–9.)

- Show my daughter's spouse what you want him to do with his life. Help him to seek your purpose for his creation. (See 1 Timothy 4:12.)

- Teach my child's spouse the basics of spiritual warfare, how to flee temptation, how to take thoughts captive, and how to stand firm against the devil's schemes. (See 1 Peter 5:8–9, 2 Corinthians 10:3–5, James 4:7–8.)

- Help my daughter's spouse to become a master of good, uplifting communication. Protect him from foul language and angry response. (See Colossians 3:8.)

- Give my child's spouse deep, satisfying personal relationships that will prepare him for marriage without compromising his purity. (See 1 Thessalonians 4:3–8.)

- Teach my daughter's spouse to be a good parent. Give his parents good parenting skills, and, if not, provide him with a godly role model. Be the Father to the fatherless if he has no father. (See Psalm 68:5–6.)

- Give my child's spouse a hunger for God through prayer and Bible study. (See Matthew 13:23.)

- Help my daughter's spouse to make a commitment to the truth, to choose honesty in every situation, even when tempted to lie to lessen punishment or consequences. (See Ephesians 4:25.)

- Give my daughter's spouse a proper attitude toward money in giving, receiving, and working. Help him learn how to budget, save, and tithe. (See 1 Timothy 6:6–11.)

- Make my child's spouse considerate and sensitive, a giving, loving Christian man who can place others needs before his own without losing his personal identity. (See 1 John 3:16–18.)[17]

Praying Specifically for the Engaged Couple

- Hope.
- Anticipation.
- Discover principles and power of covenant love.
- Equipped for marriage.
- Guidance.
- Handle stress.
- Communicate with each other in truth and love.
- Keep their focus on God.
- Listen and learn.
- Love God with their whole being.
- Maturity.
- Learn the art of deferring to one another.
- Mentors and models.
- Wisdom.
- God-centered priorities.
- Strength in the planning and beyond.
- Prepare their hearts.
- Put their trust in God.
- Transition from single to married.
- Will be united as one.
- Walk with God.
- Seek wise counsel.

Suggestions to Pray for Friends

- Trust in the Lord with all their heart.
- Be comforted.
- Live in harmony with others.
- That God's grace and love will surround them.
- Protection from the enemy.
- Blessings will be showered upon them.
- Grow in grace.
- Draw closer to God.
- Strength to overcome their battles.
- Insight and discernment.
- Encouragement.
- Rooted and grounded in Christ.
- God will guide their every step.
- Needs will be met.
- Worries, anxieties, and fears will be calmed.
- Filled with hope.
- Safety and security.
- Eyes fixed on Jesus.
- Courage for each day.
- Wisdom.
- Spiritual victory.
- Peace of God
- Hope for the future.

Suggestions to Pray for Your Adult Children

Pray that your adult child would...

- Develop a heart for God and His Word.
- Live according to biblical priorities.
- Hold to the principles of biblical marriage.
- Shepherd with grace the hearts of their children.
- Develop and maintain strong and healthy relationships.
- Grow in wisdom and discernment.
- Find employment that honors God and provides for their needs.
- Be protected from the evil one and have the strength to resist.
- Make a commitment to a local truth-preaching church.
- Live securely in their God-given identity.
- Understand the power of their words.
- Be blessed with physical health.
- Avoid all sexual pollution and temptation.
- Survive tough times.
- Experience financial stability.
- Walk with God.
- Understand God's purpose for their life.
- Have a sound mind.
- Live the "One Anothers."
- Rest.
- Experience God's forgiveness of their sins.
- Offer forgiveness to others freely.
- Live a cross-centered life.
- Join God in His kingdom work.
- Repent of and let go of difficult past experiences.
- Walk into the future God has prepared for them.
- Continue to proclaim the might of God in their years of old age.
- Find freedom, restoration, and wholeness through Christ.

Suggestions to Pray for Aging Parents

- Positive, cheerful attitudes.
- Biblical priorities.
- Blessed abundantly by God.
- Care for own soul.
- Comfort.
- Conformed to the image of Christ.
- Continue to live with an eternal focus.
- Draw closer to God.
- Exhibit fruit of the Spirit in their lives.
- Finish strong.
- Be a Godly example for children and grandchildren.
- A good name among their friends and acquaintances.
- Remain in good health.
- Remain humble.
- Live lives of integrity.
- Love God with all their being.
- Christ's love shining through them.
- Marriage relationship.
- Needs provided.
- Peace in the aging.
- Perseverance.
- Purpose during this phase of their life.
- Continue to proclaim God to future generations.
- God's power and strength in their weakness.
- Protection.
- Renewed strength and energy.
- Rest.
- Seek God.
- Strength for each day.
- Thankful for the impact they have had on others' lives.
- Trust God, even in the aging.
- Vessels of God's blessing to others.
- Walk with Jesus.
- Wisdom and discernment in all their relationships.

Suggestions to Pray for Your Pastor

- Strong character and integrity.
- Pursuit of Jesus.
- Grow in discernment.
- A strong marriage.
- A strong family.
- Joy in the middle of it all.
- Protection from Satan.
- Protection from those who have wrong motives.
- The prayers of others.
- A guarded heart.
- Meaningful friendships.
- Deep spiritual encouragement.
- Grow in humility.
- Keep a God-centered life.
- A healthy body.
- Fear God.
- Wisdom to know what to do, whatever the situation.
- Lead as a shepherd.
- Preach courageously.
- Faithful to biblical doctrine.
- That his or her ministry will be well received.
- Live out the great commission.
- Make time for prayer and worship.
- Body, mind, and spirit will be refreshed.
- Use time wisely.
- Receive a fresh anointing.
- Trust God in conflict.
- Exhibit a servant's heart.
- Be blessed with ministry team unity.
- Have clear, biblical vision.
- A heart for revival.
- The mind of Christ.
- Seek God's will.
- Work wholeheartedly.
- Growing faith.
- Financial provision and wisdom.

Praying Specifically for the Church

Pray that your church body will...

- Be constantly reminded that gospel grace is the starting point.
- Love God as Father.
- Seek the Lord.
- Honor Jesus as King.
- Follow the Holy Spirit.
- Be united.
- Form a culture of discipleship.
- Be full of goodness.
- Instruct one another.
- Be ministers of Christ.
- Fulfill the ministry of the gospel of Christ.
- Develop a culture of "linking deeply with a few."
- Strive together in prayer.
- Pursue peace.
- Be filled with all knowledge.
- Be worthy of God's calling.
- Fulfill every resolve for good and every work of faith by His power.
- Walk in a manner worthy of the Lord.
- Please God.
- Bear fruit in every good work.
- Increase in the knowledge of God.
- Be given the spirit of wisdom and of revelation in the knowledge of God.
- Invest in others.
- Abound more and more in love, with knowledge and all discernment.
- Approve what is excellent.
- Restore the broken.
- Be pure and blameless for the day of Christ.
- Be filled with the fruit of righteousness that comes through Jesus Christ.
- Choose good over evil.
- Pursue future disciples.
- View "work" as worship.
- Adhere to the Scripture in all preaching and teaching.
- Have a hunger for studying the Bible.
- Pray for their elders to be protected and remain above reproach.
- Remain singularly focused.
- Be a place of meaningful relationships.
- Choose songs that teach biblical confession, lament, and praise.
- Reflect God's heart for the generations.
- Be filled with teachers who give their responsibility proper weight.
- Be gospel peculiar, growing in distinction from the world.
- Share the gospel.
- Be prepared for persecution.

Suggestions to Pray in a Season of Transition

- Focus on what lies ahead.
- Trust God with the future.
- Keep from worry.
- Rest when needed.
- Strength for the change.
- Feel God's presence.
- Gratitude for a new opportunity.
- Calm in the anxiousness.
- God's leading.
- Past experiences.
- Future hope.
- Positive attitude.
- Wisdom in moving forward and making decisions.
- Receptive to change.
- Opportunity to be a blessing to others.
- Comfort in the unknown.
- Assurance of God's unfailing love.
- Fresh mercies.
- Transforming grace.
- Ability to give up control.
- Stay focused on Jesus.
- Give all glory to God.
- Entrust self to God's plan and purposes.
- No fear.
- Proper perspective.
- Reminded of God's deep compassion.
- Gratitude for the gifts, talents, and skills God has poured out.
- A friend to offer encouragement and accountability.
- A sense of "fun."

Suggestions to Pray in a Season of Anxiety

- A quiet mind.
- A peaceful heart.
- Release of the unknown.
- The absence of fear.
- Trust in God.
- Remind me how I have been blessed with every spiritual blessing.
- The presence of faith.
- The eyes of my heart opened.
- Strength.
- Strongholds demolished.
- Thoughts taken captive.
- Surrounded by friends and family who understand.
- Remember I am seated with Christ in the heavenly realm.
- Keep my feet from stumbling.
- Remember that God will provide everything for life, peace, and protection.
- Cast my cares upon God.
- Remember I am never alone.
- Rest in the promise of God's protection.
- Remember I need not worry or fear.
- Know that God cares for me.
- Know that I am covered by His wings.
- Remember that He who began a good work in me will be faithful to complete it.
- Remember nothing surprises my God.
- God is my perfect peace.
- Guard my heart and my mind.
- Remind me of Your resurrection power.
- Help me to stand strong in Your armor.
- Grant me time in Your word today.
- God goes before me.
- Nothing is impossible with God.
- Renew my mind.
- Remind me of truth.

Scriptures to Pray for Yourself

Knowledge of God - *And this is eternal life, that they know you, the only true God, and Jesus Christ whom you have sent* (John 17:3).

A Sense of Awe - *But will God indeed dwell on the earth? Behold, heaven and the highest heaven cannot contain you; how much less this house that I have built!* (1 Kings 8:27).

Love for God - *And you shall love the Lord your God with all your heart and with all your soul and with all your mind and with all your strength* (Mark 12:30).

True Worship - *The hour is coming, and is now here, when the true worshipers will worship the Father in spirit and truth* (John 4:23).

Love for God's Word - *How sweet are your words to my taste, sweeter than honey to my mouth!* (Psalm 119:103).

Study of God's Word - *I have stored up your word in my heart, that I might not sin against you* (Psalm 119:11).

A Praying Life - *Do not be anxious about anything, but in everything by prayer and supplication with thanksgiving let your requests be made known to God* (Philippians 4:6).

A Cross-Centered Life - *Now I would remind you, brothers, of the gospel I preached to you, which you received, in which you stand, and by which you are being saved, if you hold fast to the word I preached to you—unless you believed in vain. For I delivered to you as of first importance what I also received: that Christ died for our sins in accordance with the Scriptures, that he was buried, that he was raised on the third day in accordance with the Scriptures* (1 Corinthians 15:1-4).

Trust in the One True God - *Let me hear in the morning of your steadfast love, for in you I trust. Make me know the way I should go, for to you I lift up my soul* (Psalm 143:8).

Wisdom - *She opens her mouth with wisdom, and the teaching of kindness is on her tongue.* (Proverbs 31:26)

Pure Heart - *Blessed are the pure in heart, for they shall see God* (Matthew 5:8).

Thoughts - *Whatever is true, whatever is honorable, whatever is just, whatever is pure, whatever is lovely, whatever is commendable, if there is any excellence, if there is anything worthy of praise, think about these things* (Philippians 4:8).

Words - *Let no corrupting talk come out of your mouths, but only such as is good for building up, as fits the occasion, that it may give grace to those who hear* (Ephesians 4:29).

Marriage - *Has not the L*ORD *made them one? In flesh and spirit they are his* (Malachi 2:15, NIV1984).

Relationship with Children - *Like arrows in the hand of a warrior are the children of one's youth* (Psalm 127:4).

Relationship with Grandchildren - *Grandchildren are the crown of the aged, and the glory of children is their fathers* (Proverbs 17:6).

Time with Grandchildren - *I have been reminded of your sincere faith, which first lived in your grandmother Lois and in your mother Eunice and, I am persuaded, now lives in you also* (2 Timothy 1:5, NIV1984).

Family - *For this reason I bow my knees before the Father, from whom every family in heaven and on earth is named, that according to the riches of his glory he may grant you to be strengthened with power through his Spirit in your inner being* (Ephesians 3:14-16).

Friends - *Oil and perfume make the heart glad, and the sweetness of a friend comes from his earnest counsel* (Proverbs 27:9).

Ministry - *The whole body, joined and held together by every joint with which it is equipped, when each part is working properly, makes the body grow so that it builds itself up in love* (Ephesians 4:16).

Rest - *He makes me lie down in green pastures. He leads me beside still waters* (Psalm 23:2).

Health - *Beloved, I pray that you may prosper in all things and be in health, just as your soul prospers* (3 John 2, NKJV).

The Future - *I know the plans I have for you, declares the L*ORD*, plans for welfare and not for evil, to give you a future and a hope* (Jeremiah 29:11).

Work - *Whatever your hand finds to do, do it with your might* (Ecclesiastes 9:10).

Body - *Your body is a temple of the Holy Spirit within you* (1 Corinthians 6:19).

Aging - *Even to your old age I am he, and to gray hairs I will carry you. I have made, and I will bear; I will carry and will save* (Isaiah 46:4).

Scripture to Pray for Godly Character

Contentedness - *Not that I am speaking of being in need, for I have learned in whatever situation I am to be content* (Philippians 4:11).

Control of the Tongue - *Whoever goes about slandering reveals secrets, but he who is trustworthy in spirit keeps a thing covered* (Proverbs 11:13).

Courage - *Wait for the Lord; be strong, and let your heart take courage* (Psalm 27:14).

Dependability - *Commit your work to the Lord, and your plans will be established* (Proverbs 16:3).

Diligence - *The plans of the diligent lead surely to abundance* (Proverbs 21:5).

Discernment - *A wise man's heart discerns both time and judgment* (Ecclesiastes 8:5, NKJV).

Fearlessness - *But he said to me, "My grace is sufficient for you, for my power is made perfect in weakness." Therefore I will boast all the more gladly of my weaknesses, so that the power of Christ may rest upon me* (2 Corinthians 12:9).

Forgiveness - *Be kind to one another, tenderhearted, forgiving one another, as God in Christ forgave you* (Ephesians 4:32).

Friendship - *Finally, all of you, have unity of mind, sympathy, brotherly love, a tender heart, and a humble mind* (1 Peter 3:8).

Gentleness - *If anyone is caught in any transgression, you who are spiritual should restore him in a spirit of gentleness. Keep watch on yourself, lest you too be tempted* (Galatians 6:1).

Giving - *Give, and it will be given to you. Good measure, pressed down, shaken together, running over, will be put into your lap. For with the measure you use it will be measured back to you* (Luke 6:38).

Gratitude - *Let the word of Christ dwell in you richly…singing psalms and hymns and spiritual songs, with thankfulness in your hearts to God* (Colossians 3:16).

Hatred for Sin - *O you who love the Lord, hate evil! He preserves the lives of his saints; he delivers them from the hand of the wicked* (Psalm 97:10).

Humility - *What does the Lord require of you but to do justice, and to love kindness, and to walk humbly with your God?* (Micah 6:8).

Joy - *Ask, and you will receive, that your joy may be full* (John 16:24).

Kindness - *Be kind to one another, tenderhearted, forgiving one another, as God in Christ forgave you* (Ephesians 4:32).

Love - *We love because he first loved us* (1 John 4:19).

Mercy - *There will be no mercy for those who have shown no mercy. But if you have been merciful, then God's mercy toward you will win out over his judgment against you* (James 2:13, TLB).

Obedience - *Children, obey your parents in everything, for this pleases the Lord* (Colossians 3:20).

Passion for God - *My soul clings to you; your right hand upholds me* (Psalm 63:8).

Patience - *The Lord's servant must not be quarrelsome but kind to everyone, able to teach, patiently enduring evil* (2 Timothy 2:24).

Peace - *Seek peace and pursue it* (1 Peter 3:11).

Purity - *Flee from sexual immorality. Every other sin a person commits is outside the body, but the sexually immoral person sins against his own body. Or do you not know that your body is a temple of the Holy Spirit within you, whom you have from God? You are not your own, for you were bought with a price. So glorify God in your body* (1 Corinthians 6:18-20).

Respect for Authority - *There is no authority except from God, and those that exist have been instituted by God* (Romans 13:1).

Responsibility - *For each will have to bear his own load* (Galatians 6:5).

Self-Control - *A man without self-control is like a city broken into and left without walls* (Proverbs 25:28).

Self-Discipline - *Love not sleep, lest you come to poverty; open your eyes, and you will have plenty of bread* (Proverbs 20:13).

Selflessness - *Do not use your freedom as an opportunity for the flesh, but through love serve one another* (Galatians 5:13).

Sharing - *Do not neglect to do good and to share what you have, for such sacrifices are pleasing to God* (Hebrews 13:16).

Submission to God - *Submit yourselves therefore to God. Resist the devil, and he will flee from you* (James 4:7).

Unselfishness - *Put on then, as God's chosen ones, holy and beloved, compassionate Hearts, kindness, humility, meekness, and patience* (Colossians 3:12).

Wisdom - *The child grew and became strong, filled with wisdom. And the favor of God was upon him* (Luke 2:40).

Worship - *They said to him, "Do you hear what these are saying?" And Jesus said to them, "Yes; have you never read, 'Out of the mouths of infants and nursing babies you have prepared praise'?"* (Matthew 21:16)

Scripture Praise

Praise the Lord God for who He is.

Almighty God - *O Lord God of hosts, who is mighty as you are, O Lord, with your faithfulness all around you?* (Psalm 89:8).

The Great I AM - *Then Moses said to God, "If I come to the people of Israel and say to them, 'The God of your fathers has sent me to you,' and they ask me, 'What is his name?' what shall I say to them?" God said to Moses, "I am who I am." And he said, "Say this to the people of Israel: 'I am has sent me to you.'" God also said to Moses, "Say this to the people of Israel: 'The Lord, the God of your fathers, the God of Abraham, the God of Isaac, and the God of Jacob, has sent me to you.' This is my name forever, and thus I am to be remembered throughout all generations"* (Exodus 3:13-15).

King of Kings and Lord of Lords - *He who is the blessed and only Sovereign, the King of kings and Lord of lords* (1 Timothy 6:15).

Creator God - *You are the Lord, you alone. You have made heaven, the heaven of heavens, with all their host, the earth and all that is on it, the seas and all that is in them; and you preserve all of them; and the host of heaven worships you* (Nehemiah 9:6).

The Only God - *"I am the Lord, and there is no other, besides me there is no God; I equip you, though you do not know me"* (Isaiah 45:5).

The Holy God - *And the four living creatures, each of them with six wings, are full of eyes all around and within, and day and night they never cease to say, "Holy, holy, holy, is the Lord God Almighty, who was and is and is to come!"* (Revelation 4:8).

Everlasting Father - *For to us a child is born, to us a son is given; and the government shall be upon his shoulder, and his name shall be called Wonderful Counselor, Mighty God, Everlasting Father, Prince of Peace* (Isaiah 9:6).

The God of the Whole Earth - *For your Maker is your husband, the Lord of hosts is his name; and the Holy One of Israel is your Redeemer, the God of the whole earth he is called* (Isaiah 54:5).

My Shepherd - *The Lord is my shepherd; I shall not want. He makes me lie down in green pastures. He leads me beside still waters. He restores my soul. He leads me in paths of righteousness for his name's sake* (Psalm 23:1-3).

Our Savior - *To the only God, our Savior, through Jesus Christ our Lord, be glory, majesty, dominion, and authority, before all time and now and forever. Amen* (Jude 25).

The God of Wonders - *You are the God who works wonders; you have made known your might among the peoples* (Psalm 77:14).

My Light and My Salvation - *The LORD is my light and my salvation; whom shall I fear? The LORD is the stronghold of my life; of whom shall I be afraid?* (Psalm 27:1).

The Banner Who Leads in Triumphal Procession - *But thanks be to God, who in Christ always leads us in triumphal procession, and through us spreads the fragrance of the knowledge of him everywhere* (2 Corinthians 2:14).

My Fortress and My Refuge - *He only is my rock and my salvation, my fortress; I shall not be shaken. On God rests my salvation and my glory; my mighty rock, my refuge is God.* (Psalm 62:6-7).

Sovereign - *Yours, O LORD, is the greatness and the power and the glory and the victory and the majesty, for all that is in the heavens and in the earth is yours. Yours is the kingdom, O LORD, and you are exalted as head above all. Both riches and honor come from you, and you rule over all. In your hand are power and might, and in your hand it is to make great and to give strength to all. And now we thank you, our God, and praise your glorious name* (1 Chronicles 29:11-13).

Full of Mercy - *Nevertheless, in your great mercies you did not make an end of them or forsake them, for you are a gracious and merciful God* (Nehemiah 9:31).

Love - *So we have come to know and to believe the love that God has for us. God is love, and whoever abides in love abides in God, and God abides in him* (1 John 4:16).

Wise - *The LORD by wisdom founded the earth; by understanding he established the heavens* (Proverbs 3:19).

Healer - *"If you will diligently listen to the voice of the LORD your God, and do that which is right in his eyes, and give ear to his commandments and keep all his statutes, I will put none of the diseases on you that I put on the Egyptians, for I am the LORD, your healer"* (Exodus 15:26).

The Bearer of My Burdens - *Blessed be the Lord, who daily bears us up; God is our salvation* (Psalm 68:19).

The God Who Answers Prayer - *"Before they call I will answer; while they are yet speaking I will hear"* (Isaiah 65:24).

Justifier of the One Who Has Faith - *It was to show his righteousness at the present time, so that he might be just and the justifier of the one who has faith in Jesus* (Romans 3:26).

The God of Joy - *May the God of hope fill you with all joy and peace in believing, so that by the power of the Holy Spirit you may abound in hope* (Romans 15:13).

Deliverer - *But I am poor and needy; hasten to me, O God! You are my help and my deliverer; O Lord, do not delay!* (Psalm 70:5).

The God of Peace - *For God is not a God of confusion but of peace* (1 Corinthians 14:33).

Provider of All Things - *And God is able to make all grace abound to you, so that having all sufficiency in all things at all times, you may abound in every good work* (2 Corinthians 9:8).

Faithful - *The steadfast love of the Lord never ceases; his mercies never come to an end; they are new every morning; great is your faithfulness* (Lamentations 3:22-23).

Forgiving - *They refused to obey and were not mindful of the wonders that you performed among them, but they stiffened their neck and appointed a leader to return to their slavery in Egypt. But you are a God ready to forgive, gracious and merciful, slow to anger and abounding in steadfast love, and did not forsake them* (Nehemiah 9:17).

God of All Comfort - *Blessed be the God and Father of our Lord Jesus Christ, the Father of mercies and God of all comfort* (2 Corinthians 1:3).

Full of Grace - *[H]e predestined us for adoption to himself as sons through Jesus Christ, according to the purpose of his will, to the praise of his glorious grace, with which he has blessed us in the Beloved. In him we have redemption through his blood, the forgiveness of our trespasses, according to the riches of his grace, which he lavished upon us, in all wisdom and insight* (Ephesians 1:5-8).

The Lifter of My Head - *But you, O Lord, are a shield about me, my glory, and the lifter of my head* (Psalm 3:3).

The One Who Gave His Only Son - *For God so loved the world, that he gave his only Son, that whoever believes in him should not perish but have eternal life* (John 3:16).

Great and Beyond Our Understanding - *Behold, God is great, and we know him not; the number of his years is unsearchable* (Job 36:26).

Patient - *The Lord is not slow to fulfill his promise as some count slowness, but is patient toward you, not wishing that any should perish, but that all should reach repentance* (2 Peter 3:9).

Immeasurable - *Oh, the depth of the riches and wisdom and knowledge of God! How unsearchable are his judgments and how inscrutable his ways!* (Romans 11:33).

All-Powerful - *Ah, Lord God! It is you who have made the heavens and the earth by your great power and by your outstretched arm! Nothing is too hard for you* (Jeremiah 32:17).

Good - *You are good and do good; teach me your statutes* (Psalm 119:68).

Unchanging - *Jesus Christ is the same yesterday and today and forever* (Hebrews 13:8).

Transcendent - *The Lord is high above all nations, and his glory above the heavens!* (Psalm 113:4).

Self-sufficient - *The God who made the world and everything in it, being Lord of heaven and earth, does not live in temples made by man, nor is he served by human hands, as though he needed anything, since he himself gives to all mankind life and breath and everything* (Acts 17:24-25).

All-Knowing - *O Lord, you have searched me and known me! You know when I sit down and when I rise up; you discern my thoughts from afar. You search out my path and my lying down and are acquainted with all my ways. Even before a word is on my tongue, behold, O Lord, you know it altogether. You hem me in, behind and before, and lay your hand upon me. Such knowledge is too wonderful for me; it is high; I cannot attain it* (Psalm 139:1-6).

Unbound by Place or Time - *Where shall I go from your Spirit? Or where shall I flee from your presence? If I ascend to heaven, you are there! If I make my bed in Sheol, you are there! If I take the wings of the morning and dwell in the uttermost parts of the sea, even there your hand shall lead me, and your right hand shall hold me. If I say, "Surely the darkness shall cover me, and the light about me be night," even the darkness is not dark to you; the night is bright as the day, for darkness is as light with you* (Psalm 139:7-12).

Head of the Church - *And he put all things under his feet and gave him as head over all things to the church, which is his body, the fullness of him who fills all in all* (Ephesians 1:22-23).

Praying Scripture for Singles

Seek God with Whole Heart - With my whole heart I seek you; let me not wander from your commandments! (Psalm 119:10).

Keep Focus on God - Turn my eyes from looking at worthless things; and give me life in your ways (Psalm 119:37).

God's Will be Done - "Father, if you are willing, remove this cup from me. Nevertheless, not my will, but yours, be done" (Luke 22:42).

Delight in the Lord - Delight yourself in the Lord, and he will give you the desires of your heart. Commit your way to the Lord; trust in him, and he will act (Psalm 37:4-5).

Poured Into by Those Who Love - And he gave the apostles, the prophets, the evangelists, the shepherds and teachers, to equip the saints for the work of ministry, for building up the body of Christ, until we all attain to the unity of the faith and of the knowledge of the Son of God, to mature manhood, to the measure of the stature of the fullness of Christ, so that we may no longer be children, tossed to and fro by the waves and carried about by every wind of doctrine, by human cunning, by craftiness in deceitful schemes. Rather, speaking the truth in love, we are to grow up in every way into him who is the head, into Christ, from whom the whole body, joined and held together by every joint with which it is equipped, when each part is working properly, makes the body grow so that it builds itself up in love (Ephesians 4:11-16).

A Spirit of Wisdom and of Revelation - I do not cease to give thanks for you, remembering you in my prayers, that the God of our Lord Jesus Christ, the Father of glory, may give you the Spirit of wisdom and of revelation in the knowledge of him, having the eyes of your hearts enlightened, that you may know what is the hope to which he has called you, what are the riches of his glorious inheritance in the saints, and what is the immeasurable greatness of his power toward us who believe, according to the working of his great might (Ephesians 1:16-19).

Strength in God Alone - Whom have I in heaven but you? And there is nothing on earth that I desire besides you. My flesh and my heart may fail, but God is the strength of my heart and my portion forever (Psalm 73:25-26).

Contentment - But godliness with contentment is great gain, for we brought nothing into the world, and we cannot take anything out of the world. But if we have food and clothing, with these we will be content (1 Timothy 6:6-8).

Steadied Steps and Satisfied Completely - *Keep steady my steps according to your promise, and let no iniquity get dominion over me (Psalm 119:133).*

Glorify God in This Season of Singleness - *Now may the God of peace who brought again from the dead our Lord Jesus, the great shepherd of the sheep, by the blood of the eternal covenant, equip you with everything good that you may do his will, working in us that which is pleasing in his sight, through Jesus Christ, to whom be glory forever and ever. Amen (Hebrews 13:20-21).*

Contentment and Trust - *So to keep me from becoming conceited because of the surpassing greatness of the revelations, a thorn was given me in the flesh, a messenger of Satan to harass me, to keep me from becoming conceited. Three times I pleaded with the Lord about this, that it should leave me. But he said to me, "My grace is sufficient for you, for my power is made perfect in weakness." Therefore I will boast all the more gladly of my weaknesses, so that the power of Christ may rest upon me. For the sake of Christ, then, I am content with weaknesses, insults, hardships, persecutions, and calamities. For when I am weak, then I am strong (2 Corinthians 12:7-10).*

Grow More and More Christlike - *And it is my prayer that your love may abound more and more, with knowledge and all discernment, so that you may approve what is excellent, and so be pure and blameless for the day of Christ, filled with the fruit of righteousness that comes through Jesus Christ, to the glory and praise of God (Philippians 1:9-11).*

A Future and A Hope - *For I know the plans I have for you, declares the Lord, plans for welfare and not for evil, to give you a future and a hope (Jeremiah 29:11).*

Clarity in Dating - *Do nothing from selfish ambition or conceit, but in humility count others more significant than yourselves. Let each of you look not only to his own interests, but also to the interests of others. Have this mind among yourselves, which is yours in Christ Jesus, who, though he was in the form of God, did not count equality with God a thing to be grasped, but emptied himself, by taking the form of a servant, being born in the likeness of men. And being found in human form, he humbled himself by becoming obedient to the point of death, even death on a cross (Philippians 2:3-8).*

Grace and Contentment in This Season - *Only let each person lead the life that the Lord has assigned to him, and to which God has called him (1 Corinthians 7:17).*

Wait on the Lord - *Therefore the Lord waits to be gracious to you, and therefore he exalts himself to show mercy to you. For the Lord is a God of justice; blessed are all those who wait for him (Isaiah 30:18).*

There is A Time for Everything - *For everything there is a season, and a time for every matter under heaven: a time to be born, and a time to die; a time to plant, and a time to pluck up what is planted; a time to kill, and a time to heal; a time to break down, and a time to build up; a time to weep, and a time to laugh; a time to mourn, and a time to dance; a time to cast away stones, and a time to gather stones together; a time to embrace, and a time to refrain from embracing; a time to seek, and a time to lose; a time to keep, and a time to cast away; a time to tear, and a time to sew; a time to keep silence, and a time to speak; a time to love, and a time to hate; a time for war, and a time for peace* (Ecclesiastes 3:1-8).

Peace of God will Guard Heart and Mind - *And the peace of God, which surpasses all understanding, will guard your hearts and your minds in Christ Jesus* (Philippians 4:7).

Seek First the Kingdom of God - *But seek first the kingdom of God and his righteousness, and all these things will be added to you* (Matthew 6:33).

Love God with Heart, Soul, and Might - *You shall love the L̲o̲r̲d̲ your God with all your heart and with all your soul and with all your might* (Deuteronomy 6:5).

Scriptures to Pray for My Wife

Love the Lord - *And you shall love the Lord your God with all your heart and with all your soul and with all your mind and with all your strength (Mark 12:30).*

Holiness - *Now may the God of peace himself sanctify you completely, and may your whole spirit and soul and body be kept blameless at the coming of our Lord Jesus Christ (1 Thessalonians 5:23).*

Spiritual Maturity - *until we all attain to the unity of the faith and of the knowledge of the Son of God, to mature manhood, to the measure of the stature of the fullness of Christ, so that we may no longer be children, tossed to and fro by the waves and carried about by every wind of doctrine, by human cunning, by craftiness in deceitful schemes (Ephesians 4:13-14).*

Hope for the Future - *[H]aving the eyes of your hearts enlightened, that you may know what is the hope to which he has called you, what are the riches of his glorious inheritance in the saints, and what is the immeasurable greatness of his power toward us who believe, according to the working of his great might (Ephesians 1:18-19).*

Strengthened with Holy Spirit Power - *That according to the riches of his glory he may grant you to be strengthened with power through his Spirit in your inner being, so that Christ may dwell in your hearts through faith—that you, being rooted and grounded in love, may have strength to comprehend with all the saints what is the breadth and length and height and depth, and to know the love of Christ that surpasses knowledge, that you may be filled with all the fullness of God (Ephesians 3:16-19).*

Persistent in Prayer - *Praying at all times in the Spirit, with all prayer and supplication. To that end, keep alert with all perseverance, making supplication for all the saints (Ephesians 6:18).*

Contentment - *But godliness with contentment is great gain, for we brought nothing into the world, and we cannot take anything out of the world. But if we have food and clothing, with these we will be content (1 Timothy 6:6-8).*

Learn to Take Every Thought Captive - *We destroy arguments and every lofty opinion raised against the knowledge of God, and take every thought captive to obey Christ (2 Corinthians 10:5).*

Integrity - *Blessed are those whose way is blameless, who walk in the law of the Lord! Blessed are those who keep his testimonies, who seek him with their whole heart (Psalm 119:1-2).*

Trust in the Lord - Trust in the L ORD with all your heart, and do not lean on your own understanding. In all your ways acknowledge him, and he will make straight your paths (Proverbs 3:5-6).

Courage - Be strong and courageous. Do not fear or be in dread of them, for it is the L ORD your God who goes with you. He will not leave you or forsake you (Deuteronomy 31:6).

Discernment - But solid food is for the mature, for those who have their powers of discernment trained by constant practice to distinguish good from evil (Hebrews 5:14).

Self-Control - Do you not know that in a race all the runners run, but only one receives the prize? So run that you may obtain it. Every athlete exercises self-control in all things. They do it to receive a perishable wreath, but we an imperishable (1 Corinthians 9:24-25).

Thoughts and Actions - Finally, brothers, whatever is true, whatever is honorable, whatever is just, whatever is pure, whatever is lovely, whatever is commendable, if there is any excellence, if there is anything worthy of praise, think about these things. What you have learned and received and heard and seen in me—practice these things, and the God of peace will be with you (Philippians 4:8-9).

Clear Conscience - [H]aving a good conscience, so that, when you are slandered, those who revile your good behavior in Christ may be put to shame. For it is better to suffer for doing good, if that should be God's will, than for doing evil (1 Peter 3:16-17).

Holy Fear - Better is a little with the fear of the L ORD than great treasure and trouble with it (Proverbs 15:16).

Resist the Devil - Submit yourselves therefore to God. Resist the devil, and he will flee from you (James 4:7).

Wise Use of Time - Look carefully then how you walk, not as unwise but as wise, making the best use of the time, because the days are evil. Therefore do not be foolish, but understand what the will of the Lord is (Ephesians 5:15-17).

Nonjudgmental - Why do you see the speck that is in your brother's eye, but do not notice the log that is in your own eye? (Matthew 7:3).

Prepared for Spiritual Battle - Finally, be strong in the Lord and in the strength of his might. Put on the whole armor of God, that you may be able to stand against the schemes of the devil (Ephesians 6:10-11).

Heavenly Minded - *If then you have been raised with Christ, seek the things that are above, where Christ is, seated at the right hand of God. Set your minds on things that are above, not on things that are on earth. For you have died, and your life is hidden with Christ in God* (Colossians 3:1-3).

Perseverance - *I press on toward the goal for the prize of the upward call of God in Christ Jesus* (Philippians 3:14).

Renewed Strength - *They who wait for the L*ORD *shall renew their strength; they shall mount up with wings like eagles; they shall run and not be weary; they shall walk and not faint* (Isaiah 40:31).

Filled with the Fullness of God - *[T]hat according to the riches of his glory he may grant you to be strengthened with power through his Spirit in your inner being, so that Christ may dwell in your hearts through faith—that you, being rooted and grounded in love, may have strength to comprehend with all the saints what is the breadth and length and height and depth, and to know the love of Christ that surpasses knowledge, that you may be filled with all the fullness of God* (Ephesians 3:16-19).

Knowledge of God - *And this is eternal life, that they know you, the only true God, and Jesus Christ whom you have sent* (John 17:3).

Wisdom in Choosing Friends - *Whoever walks with the wise becomes wise, but the companion of fools will suffer harm* (Proverbs 13:20).

A Reflector of Glory - *You are the light of the world. A city set on a hill cannot be hidden. Nor do people light a lamp and put it under a basket, but on a stand, and it gives light to all in the house. In the same way, let your light shine before others, so that they may see your good works and give glory to your Father who is in heaven* (Matthew 5:14-16).

Wisdom - *[M]aking your ear attentive to wisdom and inclining your heart to understanding* (Proverbs 2:2).

Love as You Have Commanded - *Love is patient and kind; love does not envy or boast; it is not arrogant or rude. It does not insist on its own way; it is not irritable or resentful; it does not rejoice at wrongdoing, but rejoices with the truth. Love bears all things, believes all things, hopes all things, endures all things* (1 Corinthians 13:4-7).

Exhibit the Fruit of the Spirit - *But the fruit of the Spirit is love, joy, peace, patience, kindness, goodness, faithfulness, gentleness, self-control; against such things there is no law* (Galatians 5:22-23).

Virtuous - *An excellent wife who can find? She is far more precious than jewels. The heart of her husband trusts in her, and he will have no lack of gain* (Proverbs 31:10-11).

That She Would Know My Love for Her - *Let each one of you love his wife as himself, and let the wife see that she respects her husband* (Ephesians 5:33).

Respectful toward Me - *Likewise, wives, be subject to your own husbands, so that even if some do not obey the word, they may be won without a word by the conduct of their wives, when they see your respectful and pure conduct* (1 Peter 3:1-2).

Treasure Our Children - *Behold, children are a heritage from the L*ORD*, the fruit of the womb a reward* (Psalm 127:3).

Praying Scripture for Our Marriage

Our Marriage Will Glorify God - *So, whether you eat or drink, or whatever you do, do all to the glory of God* (1 Corinthians 10:31).

Together, We Will Draw Closer to God - *Draw near to God, and he will draw near to you. Cleanse your hands, you sinners, and purify your hearts, you double-minded* (James 4:8).

A Stable, Enduring Marriage - *Ah, Lord God! It is you who have made the heavens and the earth by your great power and by your outstretched arm! Nothing is too hard for you* (Jeremiah 32:17).

Our Marriage Will be a Testimony of Our Faith - *Let no one despise you for your youth, but set the believers an example in speech, in conduct, in love, in faith, in purity* (1 Timothy 4:12).

Blessing and Strength During Difficult Times - *But he said to me, "My grace is sufficient for you, for my power is made perfect in weakness." Therefore I will boast all the more gladly of my weaknesses, so that the power of Christ may rest upon me* (2 Corinthians 12:9).

Protection from Satan's Attacks - *Be sober-minded; be watchful. Your adversary the devil prowls around like a roaring lion, seeking someone to devour* (1 Peter 5:8).

Strength to Stand Strong against the Spiritual Forces that Threaten Our Faith and Our Marriage - *Finally, be strong in the Lord and in the strength of his might. Put on the whole armor of God, that you may be able to stand against the schemes of the devil. For we do not wrestle against flesh and blood, but against the rulers, against the authorities, against the cosmic powers over this present darkness, against the spiritual forces of evil in the heavenly places* (Ephesians 6:10-12).

Great Delight and Joy Will be Found in Each Other   *Let your fountain be blessed, and rejoice in the wife of your youth* (Proverbs 5:18).

Deep and Strong Friendship with Each Other - *A friend loves at all times, and a brother is born for adversity* (Proverbs 17:17).

Wisdom and Compassion in Dealing with Our In-laws - *Blessed are the merciful, for they shall receive mercy* (Matthew 5:7).

Speak the Truth in Love to Each Other - *Rather, speaking the truth in love, we are to grow up in every way into him who is the head, into Christ* (Ephesians 4:15).

Ability to Discern and Handle Hurts and Hindrances within Our Marriage - *Search me, O God, and know my heart! Try me and know my thoughts! And see if there be any grievous way in me, and lead me in the way everlasting!* (Psalm 139:23-24).

Maximize Our Strengths and Minimize Our Weaknesses - *The man gave names to all livestock and to the birds of the heavens and to every beast of the field. But for Adam there was not found a helper fit for him. So the L*ORD *God caused a deep sleep to fall upon the man, and while he slept took one of his ribs and closed up its place with flesh. And the rib that the L*ORD *God had taken from the man he made into a woman and brought her to the man. Then the man said, "This at last is bone of my bones and flesh of my flesh; she shall be called Woman, because she was taken out of Man"* (Genesis 2:20-23).

Kind, Tenderhearted, and Forgiving with Each Other - *Be kind to one another, tender-hearted, forgiving one another, as God in Christ forgave you* (Ephesians 4:32).

Each Will Exhibit a Servant's Heart toward the Other - *Even as the Son of Man came not to be served but to serve, and to give his life as a ransom for many* (Matthew 20:28).

Encourage Each Other with Our Words - *Let no corrupting talk come out of your mouths, but only such as is good for building up, as fits the occasion, that it may give grace to those who hear* (Ephesians 4:29).

Satisfied with One Another - *[A] lovely deer, a graceful doe. Let her breasts fill you at all times with delight; be intoxicated always in her love. Why should you be intoxicated, my son, with a forbidden woman and embrace the bosom of an adulteress!* (Proverbs 5:19-20).

A Heart to Seek After God All the Days of Our Lives - *O God, you are my God; earnestly I seek you; my soul thirsts for you; my flesh faints for you, as in a dry and weary land where there is no water* (Psalm 63:1).

Wisdom in Handling Our Finances - *Honor the L*ORD *with your wealth and with the firstfruits of all your produce; then your barns will be filled with plenty, and your vats will be bursting with wine* (Proverbs 3:9-10).

Protection from Pettiness and Unforgiveness in Our Relationship - *"For where two or three are gathered in my name, there am I among them." Then Peter came up and said to him, "Lord, how often will my brother sin against me, and I forgive him? As many as seven times?"* (Matthew 18:20-21).

Commitment and Surrender to Each Other - *Therefore a man shall leave his father and his mother and hold fast to his wife, and they shall become one flesh. And the man and his wife were both naked and were not ashamed* (Genesis 2:24-25).

Ability to Fulfill the Responsibilities Each Has Been Given as Husband and Wife - *Everyone to whom much was given, of him much will be required, and from him to whom they entrusted much, they will demand the more* (Luke 12:48).

Each Will Love God with Their Entire Being - *And he said to him, "You shall love the Lord your God with all your heart and with all your soul and with all your mind. This is the great and first commandment"* (Matthew 22:37-38).

We Will Love Our Neighbors as Ourselves - *And a second is like it: "You shall love your neighbor as yourself. On these two commandments depend all the Law and the Prophets"* (Matthew 22:39-40).

Contentment with Little or Much - *For we brought nothing into the world, and we cannot take anything out of the world. But if we have food and clothing, with these we will be content* (1 Timothy 6:7-8).

Love for and Obedience to God's Word - *Oh how I love your law! It is my meditation all the day* (Psalm 119:97).

Patient with Each Other; Not Jealous or Envious - *Love is patient and kind; love does not envy or boast; it is not arrogant or rude* (1 Corinthians 13:4).

Not Rude or Selfish with Each Other - *It does not insist on its own way; it is not irritable or resentful* (1 Corinthians 13:5).

Rejoice with Each Other in Truth - *It does not rejoice at wrongdoing, but rejoices with the truth* (1 Corinthians 13:6).

Love that Endures All Things - *Love bears all things, believes all things, hopes all things, endures all things* (1 Corinthians 13:7).

Love that Lasts - *Love never ends. As for prophecies, they will pass away; as for tongues, they will cease; as for knowledge, it will pass away* (1 Corinthians 13:8).

Faithful to Attendance and Service in the Local Church - *Not neglecting to meet together, as is the habit of some, but encouraging one another, and all the more as you see the Day drawing near* (Hebrews 10:25).

Scriptures to Pray for Your Children

Pray that your children will…

Know Christ as Savior - *If you confess with your mouth that Jesus is Lord and believe in your heart that God raised him from the dead, you will be saved (Romans 10:9).*

Recognize Jesus as the Name Above All Names - *Therefore God has highly exalted him and bestowed on him the name that is above every name, so that at the name of Jesus every knee should bow, in heaven and on earth and under the earth, and every tongue confess that Jesus Christ is Lord, to the glory of God the Father (Philippians 2:9-11).*

Trust in God and Lean Not on Their Own Understanding - *Trust in the Lord with all your heart, and do not lean on your own understanding. In all your ways acknowledge him, and he will make straight your paths (Proverbs 3:5-6).*

Desire a Close Relationship with Christ - *Blessed is the man who walks not in the counsel of the wicked, nor stands in the way of sinners, nor sits in the seat of scoffers; but his delight is in the law of the Lord, and on his law he meditates day and night. He is like a tree planted by streams of water that yields its fruit in its season, and its leaf does not wither. In all that he does, he prospers (Psalm 1:1-3).*

Mature in Christ - *[U]ntil we all attain to the unity of the faith and of the knowledge of the Son of God, to mature manhood, to the measure of the stature of the fullness of Christ (Ephesians 4:13).*

Be Surrounded by Godly Adults and Friends Who Will Pour into Them - *Iron sharpens iron, and one man sharpens another (Proverbs 27:17).*

Hate Sin - *O you who love the Lord, hate evil! He preserves the lives of his saints; he delivers them from the hand of the wicked (Psalm 97:10).*

Be Caught when Guilty - *It is good for me that I was afflicted, that I might learn your statutes (Psalm 119:71).*

Be Protected from the Enemy in Every Area of Life - *I do not ask that you take them out of the world, but that you keep them from the evil one (John 17:15).*

Know God Intimately - *That I may know him and the power of his resurrection, and may share his sufferings, becoming like him in his death (Philippians 3:10).*

Receive the Love of God - *See what kind of love the Father has given to us, that we should be called children of God; and so we are. The reason why the world does not know us is that it did not know him (1 John 3:1).*

Are Unashamed - *For I am not ashamed of the gospel, for it is the power of God for salvation to everyone who believes, to the Jew first and also to the Greek (Romans 1:16).*

Know Their Identity in Christ - *For this reason I bow my knees before the Father…that you, being rooted and grounded in love, may have strength to comprehend with all the saints what is the breadth and length and height and depth, and to know the love of Christ that surpasses knowledge (Ephesians 3:14, 17-19).*

Love God's Word - *Therefore I love your commandments above gold, above fine gold. Therefore I consider all your precepts to be right; I hate every false way. Your testimonies are wonderful; therefore my soul keeps them. The unfolding of your words gives light; it imparts understanding to the simple (Psalm 119:127-130).*

Develop the Discipline of Prayer - *Do not be anxious about anything, but in everything by prayer and supplication with thanksgiving let your requests be made known to God. And the peace of God, which surpasses all understanding, will guard your hearts and your minds in Christ Jesus (Philippians 4:6-7).*

Praise God - *And they said to him, "Do you hear what these are saying?" And Jesus said to them, "Yes; have you never read, "'Out of the mouth of infants and nursing babies you have prepared praise?'" (Matthew 21:16).*

Be Filled with the Knowledge of God's Will - *And so, from the day we heard, we have not ceased to pray for you, asking that you may be filled with the knowledge of his will in all spiritual wisdom and understanding (Colossians 1:9).*

Walk with the Lord, please Him, bear fruit, and grow in knowledge of God - *So as to walk in a manner worthy of the Lord, fully pleasing to him: bearing fruit in every good work and increasing in the knowledge of God (Colossians 1:10).*

Be Strengthened with All Power and Endure - *Being strengthened with all power, according to his glorious might, for all endurance and patience with joy (Colossians 1:11).*

Give Thanks to God (with Joy – see Colossians 1:11) - *Giving thanks to the Father, who has qualified you to share in the inheritance of the saints in light (Colossians 1:12).*

Wisdom in Discerning Good from Evil - *For your obedience is known to all, so that I rejoice over you, but I want you to be wise as to what is good and innocent as to what is evil (Romans 16:19).*

Protection from Stranger Danger - *Wisdom will save you from the ways of wicked men, from men whose words are perverse (Proverbs 2:12, NIV).*

Pursue righteousness, faith, love, and peace - *So flee youthful passions and pursue righteousness, faith, love, and peace, along with those who call on the Lord from a pure heart* (2 Timothy 2:22).

Guard Their Life with God's Word - *How can a young man keep his way pure? By guarding it according to your word. With my whole heart I seek you; let me not wander from your commandments! I have stored up your word in my heart, that I might not sin against you* (Psalm 119:9-11).

Not Be Conformed to Culture but Sold Out to God - *I appeal to you therefore, brothers, by the mercies of God, to present your bodies as a living sacrifice, holy and acceptable to God, which is your spiritual worship. Do not be conformed to this world, but be transformed by the renewal of your mind, that by testing you may discern what is the will of God, what is good and acceptable and perfect* (Romans 12:1-2).

Grow in Faith and Develop Christlike Values - *I have been crucified with Christ. It is no longer I who live, but Christ who lives in me. And the life I now live in the flesh I live by faith in the Son of God, who loved me and gave himself for me* (Galatians 2:20).

Exhibit the Fruit of the Spirit - *But the fruit of the Spirit is love, joy, peace, patience, kindness, goodness, faithfulness, gentleness, self-control; against such things there is no law* (Galatians 5:22-23).

Be Favored by God and Man - *And Jesus increased in wisdom and in stature and in favor with God and man* (Luke 2:52).

Submit Completely to God and Resist Satan - *Submit yourselves therefore to God. Resist the devil, and he will flee from you* (James 4:7).

Have a Responsible Attitude in All Their Relationships - *Then this Daniel became distinguished above all the other high officials and satraps, because an excellent spirit was in him. And the king planned to set him over the whole kingdom* (Daniel 6:3).

Honor Their Parents - *Honor your father and your mother, that your days may be long in the land that the Lord your God is giving you* (Exodus 20:12).

Respect Those in Authority over Them - *Let every person be subject to the governing authorities. For there is no authority except from God, and those that exist have been instituted by God* (Romans 13:1).

Have a Strong, Healthy Relationship with Their Siblings - *Concerning brotherly love you have no need for anyone to write to you, for you yourselves have been taught by God to love one another* (1 Thessalonians 4:9).

Choose Their Friends Wisely - *My son, if sinners entice you, do not consent. If they say, "Come with us, let us lie in wait for blood; let us ambush the innocent without reason"* (Proverbs 1:10-11).

Be Guided by the Holy Spirit in Choosing Their Spouse - *Do not be unequally yoked with unbelievers. For what partnership has righteousness with lawlessness? Or what fellowship has light with darkness?* (2 Corinthians 6:14).

Remain Pure Before Marriage - *Flee from sexual immorality. Every other sin a person commits is outside the body, but the sexually immoral person sins against his own body. Or do you not know that your body is a temple of the Holy Spirit within you, whom you have from God? You are not your own* (1 Corinthians 6:18-19).

Develop Discernment and Wisdom - *And God said to him, "Because you have asked this, and have not asked for yourself long life or riches or the life of your enemies, but have asked for yourself understanding to discern what is right, behold, I now do according to your word. Behold, I give you a wise and discerning mind, so that none like you has been before you and none like you shall arise after you"* (1 Kings 3:11-12).

Grow in Humility - *So if there is any encouragement in Christ, any comfort from love, any participation in the Spirit, any affection and sympathy, complete my joy by being of the same mind, having the same love, being in full accord and of one mind. Do nothing from selfish ambition or conceit, but in humility count others more significant than yourselves. Let each of you look not only to his own interests, but also to the interests of others* (Philippians 2:1-4).

Love Others with the Love of God - *Love one another with brotherly affection. Outdo one another in showing honor* (Romans 12:10).

Develop an Eternal Perspective - *For to me to live is Christ, and to die is gain* (Philippians 1:21).

Sense Your Calling and Purpose for Their Life - *Who saved us and called us to a holy calling, not because of our works but because of his own purpose and grace, which he gave us in Christ Jesus before the ages began* (2 Timothy 1:9).

Be Alert and Attentive in School - *The heart of him who has understanding seeks knowledge, but the mouths of fools feed on folly* (Proverbs 15:14).

Resist Negative Peer Pressure - *Whoever walks with the wise becomes wise, but the companion of fools will suffer harm* (Proverbs 13:20).

Be an Example Even in Their Youth - *Let no one despise you for your youth, but set the believers an example in speech, in conduct, in love, in faith, in purity* (1 Timothy 4:12)

Be Thoughtful in Their Screen Time Selections - *I will not set before my eyes anything that is worthless* (Psalm 101:3).

Use Discretion in Their Choice of Music - *It is better for a man to hear the rebuke of the wise than to hear the song of fools* (Ecclesiastes 7:5).

Learn to Watch and Pray against Life's Temptations - *Watch and pray that you may not enter into temptation. The spirit indeed is willing, but the flesh is weak* (Matthew 26:41).

And pray…

Thanks for Those Who Have Received the Gift of Salvation - *For God so loved the world, that he gave his only Son, that whoever believes in him should not perish but have eternal life* (John 3:16).

Scriptures to Pray for Grandchildren

Dear Father, I pray that: (Insert your grandchild's name)

Accept Advice - _____ *will listen to constructive criticism and correction, and through it gain understanding. (See Proverbs 15:31, 32.)*

Anger - _____ *will be quick to listen, slow to speak, and slow to become angry. (See James 1:19.)*

Anxiety - _____ *will cast all his/her anxieties and disappointments on You to experience your care for him/her. (See 1 Peter 5:7.)*

Confidence - _____ *will understand that the Lord is his/her helper and will always help him/her in every situation. (See Hebrews 13:6.)*

Compassionate - _____ *will be kind, compassionate, and forgiving to others. (See Ephesians 4:32.)*

Contentment - _____ *will learn the secret of contentment in every situation. (See Philippians 4:12.)*

Direction - _____ *will acknowledge You in all his/her ways and You will direct his/her path. (See Proverbs 3:6.)*

Friendships - _____ *will pursue righteousness, faith, love, and peace and enjoy the companionship of those who love the Lord. (See 2 Timothy. 2:22.)*

Future Mate - _____ *will find a spouse with a growing relationship with Jesus Christ. (See 2 Corinthians 6:14.)*

Generosity - _____ *will be generous and willing to share with others. (See 1 Timothy 6:18.)*

Good Listener - _____ *will be a good listener and think before he/she speaks. (See James 1:19.)*

Guard - _____ *will guard his/her heart, for it is the wellspring of his/her life. (See Proverbs 4:23.)*

Hunger for God's Word - _____ *will hunger and thirst for Your Word. (See Matthew 5:6.)*

Humility - _____ will do nothing out of selfish ambition, always thinking of others better than him-/herself. (See Philippians 2:3.)

Obedience to God - _____ will show his/her love for You by his/her obedience to You. (See John 14:15.)

Obedience to Parents - _____ will learn to obey his/her parents. (See Ephesians 6:1.)

Peace - _____ will not worry about anything, but pray about everything. (See Philippians 4:6.)

Protection from the Enemy - _____ will be alert and watch out for the temptations from the enemy, standing firm in his/her faith. (See 1 Peter 5:8, 9.)

Responsibility - _____ will learn to be responsible for his/her own actions and behavior. (See Galatians 6:5.)

Salvation - _____ will believe that Jesus loves him/her and died for his/her sins so he/she can have a personal relationship with You and enjoy eternal life. (See John 3:16.)

Security - _____ will always remember that You will never leave nor forsake him/her. (See Joshua 1:5.)

Self-control - _____ will live in this evil world with self-control, right conduct, and devotion to God. (See Titus 2:12.)

Servant's Heart - _____ will develop a servant's heart, serving wholeheartedly, as to the Lord and not men. (See Ephesians 6:7.)

Speech - _____ will keep his/her tongue from evil and keep his/her lips from lying. (See Psalm 34:13.)

Spiritual Growth - _____ will be rooted and built up in his/her faith, growing strong in the truth as he/she is taught. (See Colossians 2:7.)

Success - _____ will give You the desires of his/her heart and make all his/her plans succeed. (See Psalm 20:4.)

Thanks - _____ will learn to give thanks in everything, no matter what happens. (See 1 Thessalonians 5:18.)

Timidity/Fear - _____ will not have a spirit of fear and timidity, but the spirit of power, love, and self-discipline. (See 2 Timothy 1:7.)

Trust the Lord - _____ *will trust You with all his/her heart and not depend on his/her own understanding. (See Proverbs 3:5.)*

Wisdom - *when* _____ *needs wisdom, he/she will ask You for it, for You are waiting for him/her to ask. (See James 1:5.)*

Work Ethic - _____*will work hard and cheerfully at all he/she does, pleasing the Lord, not men. (See Colossians 3:23.)*[18]

Scriptures to Pray in a Season of Waiting

Remember...

God's Faithfulness - *The steadfast love of the LORD never ceases; his mercies never come to an end; they are new every morning; great is your faithfulness* (Lamentations 3:22-23).

God's Love - *Anyone who does not love does not know God, because God is love* (1 John 4:8).

There is a Hope - *May the God of hope fill you with all joy and peace in believing, so that by the power of the Holy Spirit you may abound in hope* (Romans 15:13).

You Are Not Alone in the Wait - *For God alone, O my soul, wait in silence, for my hope is from him. He only is my rock and my salvation, my fortress; I shall not be shaken. On God rests my salvation and my glory; my mighty rock, my refuge is God. Trust in him at all times, O people; pour out your heart before him; God is a refuge for us* (Psalm 62:5-8).

Jesus is the Way; He is the Truth - *Jesus said to him, "I am the way, and the truth, and the life"* (John 14:6).

God is Holding You - *Fear not, for I am with you; be not dismayed, for I am your God; I will strengthen you, I will help you, I will uphold you with my righteous right hand* (Isaiah 41:10).

To Thank God for What He Has Done and What He Will Do - *I will thank you forever, because you have done it. I will wait for your name, for it is good, in the presence of the godly* (Psalm 52:9).

God Hears You - *But as for me, I will look to the LORD; I will wait for the God of my salvation; my God will hear me* (Micah 7:7).

There is Hope in His Word - *I wait for the LORD, my soul waits, and in his word I hope; my soul waits for the Lord more than watchmen for the morning* (Psalm 130:5-6).

God Promises Renewed Strength to Those Who Wait - *They who wait for the LORD shall renew their strength; they shall mount up with wings like eagles; they shall run and not be weary; they shall walk and not faint* (Isaiah 40:31).

Ask for Strength and Courage in the Wait - *I believe that I shall look upon the goodness of the LORD in the land of the living! Wait for the LORD; be strong, and let your heart take courage; wait for the LORD!* (Psalm 27:13-14).

Seek the Lord in Your Wait - *The Lord is good to those who wait for him, to the soul who seeks him* (Lamentations 3:25).

Seek Truth and Knowledge - *Lead me in your truth and teach me, for you are the God of my salvation; for you I wait all the day long* (Psalm 25:5).

God's Blessing Comes through Times of Waiting - *He has made everything beautiful in its time. Also, he has put eternity into man's heart, yet so that he cannot find out what God has done from the beginning to the end* (Ecclesiastes 3:11).

He is the God of Perfect Timing - *The least one shall become a clan, and the smallest one a mighty nation; I am the Lord; in its time I will hasten it* (Isaiah 60:22).

Draw Strength from the Promises of God - *For all the promises of God find their Yes in him. That is why it is through him that we utter our Amen to God for his glory* (2 Corinthians 1:20).

God is Sovereign - *Which he will display at the proper time—he who is the blessed and only Sovereign, the King of kings and Lord of lords* (1 Timothy 6:15).

Trust Him - *Trust in the Lord with all your heart, and do not lean on your own understanding. In all your ways acknowledge him, and he will make straight your paths* (Proverbs 3:5-6).

Pray for Protection against Discouragement - *Have I not commanded you? Be strong and courageous. Do not be frightened, and do not be dismayed, for the Lord your God is with you wherever you go* (Joshua 1:9).

Look Back at What God Has Done in Your Life - *And you shall remember the whole way that the Lord your God has led you these forty years in the wilderness, that he might humble you, testing you to know what was in your heart, whether you would keep his commandments or not* (Deuteronomy 8:2).

Draw Near to God in the Wait - *Draw near to God, and he will draw near to you. Cleanse your hands, you sinners, and purify your hearts, you double-minded* (James 4:8).

Don't Do Life Alone - *Bear one another's burdens, and so fulfill the law of Christ* (Galatians 6:2).

Learn to Rest - *"Be still, and know that I am God. I will be exalted among the nations, I will be exalted in the earth!"* (Psalm 46:10).

NOTES

PART 1

1 Taken from *My Utmost for His Highest* by Oswald Chambers, edited by James Reimann, © 1992 by Oswald Chambers Publications Assn., Ltd., and used by permission of Discovery House Publishers, Grand Rapids MI 49501. All rights reserved (wording provided), 291.

2 Excerpt from Jennifer Kennedy Dean, *Live a Praying Life*, (c) 2011 Jennifer Kennedy Dean. Published by New Hope Publishers, an imprint of Iron Stream Media. All rights reserved. Used by Permission (wording provided), 46.

3 Dean, *Live a Praying Life*, 59.

4 Taken from *The Prayer Life* by Andrew Murray, 2.

5 Taken from *The Prayer of the Lord* by R.C. Sproul, (Reformation Trust Publishing, 2009), Used by Permission, 13.

6 Taken from "5 Great Books on Prayer" by Tim Challies, (http://www.challies.com/recommendations/prayer).

7 Taken from "10 Things I Prayed for My Children and Grandchildren Today" by Pat Layton, (http://patlayton.net/my-morning-prayers-for-my-children-and-grandchildren/).

8 Anonymous Quote

9 Taken from *Purpose in Prayer* by E.M. Bounds, 9.

10 James C. Dobson, PhD, and James C. Dobson. "Chapter 1 Understanding the Nature of Children," *Complete Marriage and Family Home Reference Guide*. (Carol Stream, IL: Tyndale, 2000), 8-9.

PART 2

11 Excerpt from Sharon Hoffman, *A Car Seat in My Convertible?* © 2008 Sharon Hoffman. Published by New Hope Publishers, an imprint of Iron Stream Media. All rights reserved. Used by permission. (Wording provided), 45.

12 Taken from *Praying in Color: Drawing a New Path to God* by Sybil MacBeth, (Brewster, MA: Paraclete Press, 2013), 19-23.

13 MacBeth, *Praying in Color*, 29-38.

14 Taken from "15 Ways to Practice 1 Thessalonians 5:17" by Cheri Gamble, (http://cheri37526.wordpress.com/2014/06/04/pray-continually-15-ways-to-practice-1-thessalonians-517/), March 14, 2018.

PART 3

15 Church of England, 1928 Book of Common Prayer. 831.

16 Pamela, Dowd, taken from "12 Ways to Pray for Your Child's Future Mate", (https://www.reviveourhearts.com/articles/12-ways-to-pray-childs-future-mate/), March 6, 2018.

17 Lillian Penner, taken from "Suggestions to Pray for Different Stages of Life, (http://www.grandparenting-withapurpose.com/free-resources/), March 5, 2018.

18 Lillian Penner, taken from "Suggestions to Pray for Grandchildren", (http://www.grandparentingwithapurpose.com/free-resources/), March 5, 2018.

Notes & Prayers

Notes & Prayers

Notes & Prayers

Notes & Prayers